Taking

World

Francis and Edith Schaeffer

Rachel Lane

CF4•K

10 9 8 7 6 5 4 3 2 1

Copyright © 2019 Rachel Lane

Paperback ISBN: 978-1-5271-0300-9
epub ISBN: 978-1-5271-0349-8
mobi ISBN: 978-1-5271-0350-4

Published by
Christian Focus Publications, Geanies House, Fearn, Tain,
Ross-shire, IV20 1TW, Scotland, U.K.
www.christianfocus.com
email: info@christianfocus.com

Printed and bound by Nørhaven, Denmark
Cover design by Daniel van Straaten

Taking on the World

Contents

For Nathan, Charis, Lydia & Phoebe

Acknowledgements

I want to thank my mother, Judi Griffiths, for introducing me to the books of the Schaeffers, several of which could be found on our family bookshelves. She had become interested in the work of the Schaeffers after hearing Francis speak at a Christian mission while she was at the University of York in 1967.

During the writing of this book I have had the privilege of speaking with Susan Schaeffer Macaulay and her daughter Fiona Macaulay Fletcher, both of whom you will encounter among its pages. I would like to thank them both for taking the time to read the manuscript and for sharing their own personal memories. Of course, any mistakes or inaccuracies are my own.

A Meeting of Minds

Two young girls entered the church building together that Sunday evening. Both were smartly dressed in outfits their mothers had made from fashionable patterns. Both wore their hair up, smooth and neatly styled for the occasion. It may have been just an ordinary Sunday evening meeting at church, but it had become the social highlight of the week. More exciting perhaps than the meeting itself was the open invitation to Sally's place after for hot chocolate and cookies, music and lively conversation.

The two girls were becoming good friends; but their minds were on very different things as they scanned the room that evening. The taller of the two was looking out for friends to wave to, wondering who would be at Sally's later, and hoping her high heeled shoes made her legs look longer. Beside her, slim and petite but with a serious expression on her pretty face, Edith Seville was looking for one person in particular: the speaker of the evening, Ed Broom. Everyone knew he had left the Presbyterian Church to join a Unitarian Church, and

Edith was very worried about the message he would deliver that night. She felt sure it would go against the truth of the Bible and all she believed in. But Edith wasn't one to sit quietly by and allow that to happen. No; she was ready for a fight, if necessary!

The girls shuffled into a seat near the back as a young man stood up to introduce the speaker and the title of his talk – "How I know that Jesus is not the Son of God, and how I know that the Bible is not the Word of God"! Edith silently fumed. This was worse than she'd feared. As Ed delivered his eloquent speech, she was already formulating a response in her head. Edith's parents had been missionaries and she had picked up lots of things from listening to the conversations between them and their friends. Her Christian faith was an important part of her life – the most important part. Indeed, although she was only seventeen, Edith already felt a deep call upon her life. She didn't know what God wanted her to do, or where, or with whom, but she knew one thing about her future: she expected always to be defending the truth.

As Ed's talk drew to a close, Edith jumped to her feet with her carefully formulated argument. But before she could open her mouth to speak, the sound of a quiet, steady voice stopped her in her tracks. A young man several rows in front of her had beaten her to it. He was short, but well built, with light brown hair. Although she could only see him from behind, Edith felt sure she had never seen him before. She quickly sat down and listened curiously to what he had to say. He spoke well, his voice gentle but firm.

"You will all think that what I am going to say is influenced by my Bible teacher at Hampden-Sydney College, whom you would think old-fashioned," he said, calmly. "He teaches that the Bible is the Word of God, and that's what I believe too. I want to say that I know Jesus is the Son of God. He is also my Savior, and has changed my life. I may not be able to answer all the things Ed has said – not yet anyway – but I want you to know just where I stand."

As he spoke, Edith nudged her friend Ellie and leaned towards her.

"Who's that?" she whispered, incredulously. "I didn't know there was anyone in this church who would defend the Bible like that."

"That's Fran Schaeffer," Ellie whispered back, knowingly. "His parents don't want him to be a pastor so they're making it really hard for him. But he's gone off to college anyway."

Edith's respect for the bold young man grew instantly and she felt a burst of compassion for him. Having only ever known loving support and encouragement from her own parents, she felt an urge to somehow comfort this poor boy. But then she realized he had finished speaking and quickly pulled her mind back to the truth at stake. Jumping to her feet once more, she eagerly reeled off her defence of the Bible, based on ideas and quotations she had picked up from books, lectures and conversations at home.

The whole room had turned round to look at this passionate, impressive young lady, and Fran Schaeffer craned his neck to get a better look at her. Petite and dark-haired, almost Mediterranean looking, the maturity of her words seemed at odds with her pretty, youthful appearance. One thing was for sure; she was definitely not one of the girls he'd met in Sunday school.

"Who on earth is that girl?" he whispered to his friend Dick, sitting beside him. "I didn't know anyone in this church knew that kind of thing!"

Dick chuckled. "That's Edith Seville," he told his friend. "She's just moved here from Toronto, Canada. Her parents used to be missionaries in China."

When Edith had said her piece, the leader of the meeting hastily announced the last hymn to avoid any further discussion. Once the singing had finished it was the end of the meeting and onto Sally's house for the two girls. Edith had mixed feelings as she got her things together to leave. She had enjoyed the buzz of lively debate, and felt rather sorry it was over. Going to Sally's would be fun, and she was glad she was starting to make new friends in Germantown at last; but the conversation did often seem a bit silly and trivial. Sometimes she felt so different from the other young people her age; so much more serious, somehow. She loved to go out, to dance and enjoy herself with the rest. But sometimes her heart ached for something deeper, something that mattered.

As she stood to join her friends, Edith suddenly saw Dick and Fran pushing through the crowd in her direction. Blushing, her eyes met Fran's steady gaze and she realized that they were definitely coming to speak to her.

Dick spoke first. "Edith, I want to introduce you to Fran Schaeffer. Fran, this is Edith Seville."

Fran smiled warmly as he shook her hand.

"May I walk you home?" he asked immediately.

Edith was momentarily torn. She had already told Ellie she'd be there that evening, and she didn't like to break a commitment.

"I'm sorry," she said, regretfully, "but I already have a date."

Fran was not to be deterred. "Break it," he urged.

Slightly taken aback, after a moment Edith found herself nodding.

"Well … yes, alright, I will," she replied slowly.

She felt such a strong desire to talk to someone who not only believed as she did but also had the courage to say so. Although he was perhaps somewhat unexceptional in appearance, Fran had already made quite an impression on her. She couldn't wait to find out more about this intriguing young man.

Outside in the warm air of a balmy summer's evening, the group dispersed. Ellie and the others began to drift off towards Sally's place, though not without a few meaningful backward glances. Fran and Edith looked at one another shyly before beginning to walk, at a leisurely pace, towards her own home. Yet after the first few moments of awkwardness, the conversation between them flowed easily as the pair began to speak of the faith they shared.

Edith was delighted to come across someone so like-minded. She had been on a few dates before, but not like this. Her mind flitted back to the senior prom at her high school, and the boy who had taken her – the perfect escort, tall, dark and handsome. She had worn a stylish green lace dress her mother had made from a Vogue pattern, which looked far more expensive than it was, adorned with the orchid her date had brought her. She should have felt like a fairy tale princess as he led her around the dance floor. And yet, somehow, it had fallen short of being the perfect evening she had hoped for. A little part of Edith had felt as though she were merely acting in a play.

This was different. Fran's love for Jesus was evident in everything he said, not to mention the tone of his voice as he spoke passionately about what he believed. He fully shared Edith's conviction that the Bible was the Word of God, complete and infallible. He shared her concern about the liberal theology that was advancing in the church, casting doubt on the historical accuracy of parts of Scripture and leading many away from the truth. While Edith had found it so hard to talk about "serious" things – like the gospel – with other boys, with Fran it was completely natural. Both of them found it refreshing to speak to someone else of their own age who was equally committed to serving Christ. So often they felt that they were having to defend their faith to others.

All too soon, they arrived at Edith's home on Ashmead Place. How strange, Fran thought, that she should live on this street! Perhaps one day soon he would have the chance to share with her what had happened to him two years ago, just a few hundred yards from this very spot.

"Well, this is me," Edith said rather reluctantly. "Thank you for walking me home."

"May I call on you again?" Fran asked, quickly, before he could stop himself. "I'm working ... a holiday job ... but maybe one day this week, when my shift ends?"

Edith nodded, feeling her cheeks warm a little. "I'd like that."

"Well ... good night then."

"Good night."

Fran waited at the gate and watched as Edith walked up the path towards her front door. He couldn't help but admire her neat, slender figure as she walked away from him, turning to give a quick wave before she closed the door behind her. He couldn't help but wonder about the family that would be greeting her now as she returned home, perhaps a little earlier than they'd expected. He tried to picture what her parents might look like. Missionaries – to China! It was funny, he thought to himself, that he and this surprising girl should find they had so much in common, when their backgrounds could hardly be more different.

Fran

It was the middle of the night, on January, 30th 1912, that Francis August Schaeffer IV had made his appearance in the world – the first and only child of Frank and Bessie Schaeffer, an honest and hardworking couple who had married and set up home together in Germantown, Philadelphia.

"That's it. I'm only having one," Bessie had told Frank firmly. "I am not going to be a slave to children!"

She shuddered to think of having a life like her own mother, who had pretty much turned their own home into a laundry to support herself and her four growing children after losing her husband. When Bessie thought back to growing up in that house she remembered the grind of constant hard work; helping her mother start the washing before school, doing the ironing after, being forced to study by gaslight long into the evening. Having to rub other people's dirty laundry by hand till her knuckles grew raw from the ribs on the washboard. Nothing but drudgery, day after day, in order to put food on the table for all those hungry little mouths!

No, she thought bitterly, life would not be like that for her family. Frank earned a decent living and they'd scrimped and saved to buy and furnish their home. One child would be plenty to share it with.

That was all right with Frank. He determined to be as good a father as he could to this fine baby boy. Having lost his own father at the tender age of three, Frank had no role model to emulate, but he had a pretty good idea what he wanted to do for his boy. He wanted to show him how to make things, teach him all the different kinds of practical skills he himself had worked hard to acquire. He would teach him the value of an honest day's work, and how to be careful with money. He would give him the chance to have an education too – something that for Frank had been cut sadly short by the need to support his family. Not education for its own sake, Frank thought to himself, but so that young Francis could do something useful with his life. Maybe, one day, he could become an engineer and make his mother proud.

Yet aside from all these ambitions, Frank also wanted to see that the boy had an easier childhood than his own, with a bit of time for holidays and fun and just … being a child. It was something neither he nor his wife had ever had.

On a bright Friday afternoon in early summer, an observant passerby might have noticed a small boy peering over the picket fence of his front garden, looking out for any sign of his Pop returning home from work.

Fridays in the Schaeffer home meant one thing: cleaning day! There was a particular job for every day of the week: as well as cleaning on Friday, there was washing on Monday, ironing on Tuesday, mending on Wednesday, and shopping on Thursday. The boy's mother worked hard all week long to keep their household in perfect order. And when Bessie Schaeffer cleaned, she meant business! Up went the hair under a large handkerchief as she dusted and polished, washed baseboards and brushed carpets until the place was spotless.

When young Fran had returned home from school, it hadn't been long before his mother shooed him out the door again – thrusting a jam sandwich into his hand to keep him going till supper.

"Out you go!" she ordered, briskly, though not unkindly. "Mrs. Cooper called this morning, prattling on and on till I thought she'd never leave! I'm so behind I'll never get finished before your Pop gets home. Especially not with you under my feet."

Fran wasn't sorry to be out of the way of all the bustle and rushing around indoors. It was too nice an afternoon for all that. The sun was high in an almost cloudless blue sky; the air warm but not uncomfortable. He felt quite content as he sat on the little lawn in front of the house, munching on his sandwich. The only trouble was, once the sandwich had gone, there wasn't really a whole lot to do in the garden. It was a tiny plot, though well kept and attractively bordered with flower beds. In one corner was the lilac bush, under which Fran used to sit spooning earth into a little pail, often displeasing his mother by getting his white socks dirty. But he had rather outgrown that activity now, and would have liked another boy to throw a ball around with … or at least a dog to play with. His mother rarely allowed playmates back to the house, however; and a pet of his own was an unlikely daydream.

Instead, Fran whistled to himself, and thought, and waited for his father to come home from work. At least it was Friday, with the weekend to look forward to; and on an afternoon like this, there might even be ice cream after dinner!

At last the familiar figure of his father rounded the corner of their road, and Fran called out merrily, "Pop! Hey, Pop!"

Frank Schaeffer, tired and dirty from a hard day's work, looked up and smiled as he saw his son leaning over the gate to greet him. When he smiled, his weathered face lit up and his blue eyes twinkled. "Hello, son."

They walked up the garden path together companionably, but before they got to the door Fran hung back a little. He had an idea he wanted to put to his father alone, without any interference from his mother!

"Pop? Might we start painting, tomorrow, do you think?" Fran gestured pointedly to the front of the house, which he felt was beginning to look in need of a bit of brightening up. "We should do the house again, really."

Fran always enjoyed the times when he was allowed to help his father with practical work around the house. Last summer, in spite of his mother's objections, he'd spent days up a ladder with a little paintbrush of his own as they repainted the exterior walls together.

Frank grinned, pleased by his son's enthusiasm.

"We'll see, lad. I'm sure there'll be something you can help me out with."

And then, as they entered the house together to the smell of onions cooking, thoughts of the next day's work gave way to thoughts of today's supper.

A few years later, and a different supper was cooking on the stove; a nice bit of steak, a rare treat to celebrate. Sitting at the table, Frank Schaeffer reached for the small cup his son had brought home and examined it proudly. He read the inscription to himself: "Pyramid Club Cup Four Minute Speech Contest, Won by Francis A. Schaeffer, Troop 38, 1923."

"Well done, son," he said, with a satisfied nod. "Well done."

Fran beamed with pleasure. He was enjoying the Scouts, having joined only that year, and felt particularly proud of winning the contest since he was at least a year younger than all the others. There had been a lot of new beginnings for Fran that year. The beginning of his time at Roosevelt Junior High School. The beginning of Scouts. The beginning of learning to swim and doing gymnastics. The beginning, even, of music lessons ... although that experience had been less successful and swiftly abandoned. Still, life was starting to open up a little bit for Fran; and at least he had a clear idea of what he was working towards. Now he could focus on the subjects he knew his parents valued – mechanical drawing, woodwork, electrical construction, and metal work. Subjects that built on all the work they'd done together at home. Subjects that might prepare him for being an engineer one day, which was still Frank's ambition for his son.

As for Fran's own ambitions ... well, no one had exactly asked him about that, but it didn't occur to him to mind. He was just living from day to day. He didn't know what he wanted from life, and nor did he know what life might have to offer him, beyond that little world of school and home and sport and Scouts.

As Bessie Schaeffer busied herself in the kitchen preparing the meal, Frank cleared his throat and leaned forward in his chair.

"Look, Fran," he said, abruptly. "I've been thinking. You should choose a new church. Any one you want to go to."

Fran was rather surprised. He knew his father had few positive things to say about church. Although Frank had been involved with the Lutheran church as a young boy, he had felt no connection with anyone there, and found no concern there for a fatherless family in need. "They were all rich kids," he used to say bitterly. "And the pastor didn't know what work was; he just stood up there and talked."

Still, Fran had often heard his friends talking about the church his Scout troop was connected with, so he could answer quite easily.

"I think I'd like to go to the First Presbyterian Church, Pop."

With a brusque nod from his father, the matter was settled.

So Fran added church attendance to his list of extracurricular activities, which over the next few years expanded to include joining the rifle club, basketball and roller skating; and then eventually a series of different Saturday jobs, from selling fish, to de-scaling steam boilers, delivering ice and even selling beaded flower pins that he taught his mother and his friends to make. Fran was energetic and involved in many things, but as he advanced through his teenage years there was a sense of restlessness. His grades were only average. He felt unmotivated, as though he were merely going through the motions of life, almost in a robotic way. Nothing really excited him.

The day all that began to change was a day like any other. An ordinary Saturday, with errands to be run. Well, perhaps not completely ordinary, as it wasn't every Saturday that found seventeen-year-old Fran making his way to the heart of downtown Philadelphia, to Leary's famous bookstore. It was a splendid, three storey building, with a mezzanine on the third floor that allowed customers to see down below and get a sense of the sheer number of books loaded onto the shelves that lined the walls of the store. As well as the shelves there were tables dotted everywhere with stacks of dusty used books for customers to peruse, but Fran didn't have time for all that. He wasn't there to browse but for a particular reason: to find an easy reading book that would be suitable for a Russian immigrant he had been helping learn to read in English. Once he had found something suitable, Fran waited for what felt like an age at the busy sales desk for someone to serve him before he could take his package and be on his way.

However, when Fran boarded the trolley car home and unwrapped his purchase, he discovered that the wrong book had been given to him. With all the chaos of the front desk and numerous customers being seen to at once, somehow they had sent him away with a book of Greek philosophy, of all unlikely things!

"Oh, for goodness' sake!" Fran said aloud to himself. It was too late to go back now. With no other distraction to be had on the ride home, he reluctantly opened the book. Having long since bypassed the more academic subjects in favor of the practical pursuits his parents valued, philosophy was completely unknown territory. Yet, as he read, he found his interest being stirred. And when, just a few days later, he finished the book, he found he wanted more. Over the next few weeks Fran became reacquainted with the library, and read more and more philosophy. Every evening he waited until his parents were asleep, not wanting to risk their questions or their disapproval – and then he would turn on his light again and read long into the night!

Fran had, quite unexpectedly, discovered his passion. He later described feeling as though a fire had been lit in his bones![1] Thinking about the meaning and purpose of life: now here was something that excited him. Yet as time went on, reflecting on his reading, Fran still felt unsatisfied. Philosophy helped him to think about questions he had never thought to ask before, but it gave him few answers.

He began to listen more attentively to the sermons he heard preached on a Sunday, but found no answers there either. In fact, the pastor's words were less inspiring than the books he was reading; he didn't seem to engage with any of the big questions Fran was asking, and it was far from clear where he got his ideas from. Fran wondered whether it was time to stop going to church for good; there was nothing for him there.

One night, long after his parents had retired to bed, Fran was reading his way through Ovid when a thought suddenly occurred to him. He realized he had never read much of the Bible for himself; and that if he was going to reject Christianity completely he should at least make sure he knew what he was rejecting. He decided, pretty much on a whim, that he would do it:

---

1. Interview with Susan Schaeffer Macaulay, June 2018.

he would read the whole Bible! After that he could stop going to church with a clear conscience.

The following evening, Fran waited as usual for his parents to turn in for the night. When he heard his father call out, "Good night, Fran", he quickly replied, "Good night!" and lay there quietly in the darkness for a few more minutes listening to the familiar bedtime sounds of running water, low voices, and eventually, the final click of their bedroom door. Then he flicked his own light back on and reached for the Bible; his own copy, barely opened. Knowing of no other way to read it, Fran turned straight to Genesis, the very first book of the Bible. And as he read, something quite remarkable began to happen. Fran found the answers he had been looking for; in the last place he had expected to find them.

He read of a Creator God who had made the world out of nothing. He read of how, with powerful words, this God brought all created things into being: earth and sky, land and sea, sun and moon, birds and creatures of the sea, animals and finally, mankind, whom he created "in His own image." He read of the task God gave them, to rule over the earth He had made. He read of the special, intimate relationship Adam and Eve had enjoyed with God, before everything went wrong and sin entered that perfect world – so that nothing would ever be the same again. He read of how the man and woman God had made doubted His goodness, rejected His rule and disobeyed the one command He had given them. And Fran didn't stop there, but continued to read the whole Bible as he had pledged. He would later describe it as though each of his questions was a balloon in the sky, and as he read through the Bible gradually the balloons were being popped.[2] One by one, Fran's questions were being answered; and they were answers that truly made sense of what he knew of the world and of himself.

No one knew of his reading. No one helped him to understand what he was reading. And when Fran gradually accepted Jesus Christ as his Lord and Savior, over the next few months, there was no one he thought he could tell. When he thought of his pastor, and the people at church who called themselves Christians, they seemed to have nothing to do with the things he was reading in this extraordinary book. So he didn't think of himself as a Christian, at first. He felt instead that he had discovered truth no one else knew about.

For a while things continued in much the same way, on the outside. Fran finished high school and was headed for the Drexel Institute to study engineering, just as his father had always wished. But anyone looking closely might have been mystified by some subtle changes in Fran and his lifestyle. They might have wondered why, in the last few months of high school, the standard of his work had markedly improved. They might have wondered why he took himself off to an

2. Ibid.

art gallery for the first time, or why he lingered in the woods. They might also have noticed that for a practical sort of person, Fran seemed to spend an awful lot of his free time in the library. Something had definitely changed.

Changing Course

One humid August evening, Fran wandered down the main street of Germantown feeling rather downhearted. The discoveries he was making in the Bible were exciting, but he had no one to share them with. Besides that, he was still looking for a job for the summer, and with the Great Depression underway, there was little work to be had. True, he had his studies at the Drexel Institute to look forward to; but if he was honest, even that thought didn't encourage him. His future course seemed to be all mapped out for him, but in his heart Fran found himself less and less certain about it.

As he made his way aimlessly along Germantown Avenue, thinking about these things, Fran eventually came to an empty plot on the corner of Ashmead Place, where a large tent had been pitched. He paused to wipe away the sweat that had gathered on his brow and to roll up his shirt sleeves; the stifling heat showed no sign of abating, even at this hour. As he rested for a moment, Fran heard coming from the tent the sound of hymns being bashed out on a piano and hearty singing. "What on earth is going on in there?" he wondered.

Fran gingerly pushed the tent flap to one side and peered in to see wooden benches in rows either side of a sawdust aisle. As he quietly entered, the singing came to an end and an Italian American man at the front rose to his feet to address the congregation. He started off by quoting a verse from the Bible, John 8:32: "And ye shall know the truth, and the truth shall make you free." From there he described how he had heard about Jesus Christ while he was serving time in prison.

"And I discovered, in the Lord Jesus, the only way out of the real prison I was in … the prison of my slavery to sin!" he declared, in his strong Italian accent.

Fran found his heart beating faster as he slid into a seat at the back to hear more. This was something quite different to the sermons about good deeds his pastor preached each week. He listened attentively as the man continued to speak, reeling off one Bible verse after another as though from memory. In front of Fran, a man leaned across to his neighbor and said in a loud whisper: "They call him 'the walking Bible'! The man knows literally hundreds of verses by heart."

The more he listened, the more excited Fran felt. He realized that the message this man was proclaiming was truly the message of the Bible as he himself had understood it. This man believed as he believed! At the end of the sermon there was an invitation for those who wanted to know the Lord Jesus to come forward for special prayer.

"Brothers and sisters, this gospel of salvation is available to every one of you. This very night, if you will just turn from your sin and cling to the cross of the Savior Jesus Christ, you can have the gift of eternal life! For the book of Romans, chapter 10, verse 9 tells us 'that if thou shalt confess with thy mouth the Lord Jesus, and shalt believe in thine heart that God hath raised him from the dead, thou shalt be saved'!"

Fran didn't hesitate to make his way down the sawdust aisle with the other new believers that night. He received Jesus as his Savior, and afterwards rushed home with a full heart and a new certainty about the way ahead. Before he slept that night, Fran recorded this most significant event in his diary: "August 19, 1930 – Tent Meeting, Anthony Zeoli – have decided to give my whole life to Christ unconditionally."[1]

Fran went back to the tent meeting again three days later, and a few days after that took several others with him, keen to share this "good news" with others. His new-found faith wasn't something that stayed in the background, like a hobby or interest, but something that forced him to look at the whole of his life in a different way. Within a month of those tent meetings, Fran found himself speaking with his old Sunday school teacher Mr. Moore about the possibility of going into

---

1. Edith Schaeffer, *The Tapestry* (Word Books, 1981), p.55.

Christian ministry. Now that he had come to know Jesus for himself, Fran felt a strong call to spend his life telling others about him. But he had so much to learn – things that he could never learn in night classes at the Drexel Institute. Another churchman, a local headmaster named Mr. Osborne, recommended that Fran consider going to Hampden-Sydney College in Virginia, as preparation for theological study later on.

But what to do about his parents? Fran knew only too well what they thought of ministers; that they were parasites who weren't earning an honest living. Because they had no time for the message of the Bible and gave no thought to spiritual things, naturally they didn't see the point of those who made a living preaching and teaching to others.

"What am I going to do, Sam?" Fran asked a friend, miserably. Sam Chestnut was another believer from the First Presbyterian Church who had recently offered Fran work at his grocery store. "I know the Bible says it's right to honor thy father and mother. It will break Pop's heart if I do this. But I feel so strongly that my Heavenly Father is calling me towards the ministry!"

"Let's keep praying about it," said Sam, sensibly.

As he continued to pray and talk with others about what to do, Fran enrolled in night classes at the Drexel Institute, as planned, taking a course in Mechanical Engineering. But his heart wasn't in it. Only a few months later, on January 30th, Fran made the decisive change he had been praying over. He withdrew from the Drexel Institute and enrolled at the Central High School, where he could take evening courses such as German and Latin and prepare to go to Hampden-Sydney College as a ministerial student.

His parents reacted to the news with as much hostility as Fran had feared. He tried to explain the message of the Christian faith to his parents, but they didn't want to listen. He felt almost as though he was speaking in a different language. Talking about "ideas" was simply not something that was done in the Schaeffer home; they were practical people. As he tried to share his increasing joy and excitement about Christian ministry, they stared at him as though he had become a stranger to them. For his part, Frank Schaeffer felt as though all his hopes for his son had been shattered. He had envisaged Fran growing up to be a working man like himself, staying close by – maybe even on the same street. Working with his hands, doing something useful – not like this.

When the day finally came for Fran to pack his trunk to leave for college that September, he did so in the chill atmosphere of a tense and silent house. He used an old wooden box as a trunk, which he had taken down to the cellar and painted a battleship grey, using a can of paint that had been left over from painting the kitchen floor. His parents hadn't bought him anything he might need, like new clothes or sports equipment, towels or bedding. In fact, his mother dealt with the situation by ignoring it; stony-faced, she went around the house that day as if no packing were going on at all. Eventually, once Fran had packed most of his normal clothing, his gym clothes and his raincoat, his mother marched into the room with her lips tightly pressed together and threw a few old towels and a cake of soap on top, without a word.

Before he went to bed that night, Frank Schaeffer appeared in the doorway of his son's bedroom and looked at the packed trunk with its lid now carefully screwed down. All he said was, "Get up in time to see me before I go to work tomorrow. 5:30."

When Fran stumbled down the stairs the following morning, bleary-eyed, he found his father standing by the front door waiting for him. For what seemed like an eternity, they looked at one another. And then his father said, "I don't want a son who is a minister, and – I don't want you to go."

Fran had always known that leaving wouldn't be easy, but he hadn't expected to face this direct challenge, this very morning. He did the only thing he could think of doing, and in a tight voice, asked, "Pop, give me just a few minutes to go down to the cellar and pray."

Down in the cellar, Fran wept and prayed. He wept not only for the pain he felt in having to disappoint his father, but in grief at his father's hardness of heart. How he longed for his father to understand, and to come to know the truth for himself! Yet his conviction was unchanged: he knew this was what God was calling him to. He had been living in the darkness, ignorant of God, for seventeen years. Looking back, he felt as though all that time he had been walking in a mist. Now that he knew the God of the Bible, life made sense. With all his heart, he wanted to give his life to proclaiming the truth and defending the truth of the Bible.

So he returned upstairs, a few minutes later, to tell his father, "Pop ... I've got to go."

His father gave him a long, hard look and then went out, going to slam the door behind him. Yet, in the final moment before it banged in its frame, his parting comment came back, "I'll pay for the first half year ... "

Reeling, Fran returned to his bedroom. The moment he walked in his eyes immediately fell upon a text he had stuck up on his wall several months earlier: "But as for me and my house, we will serve the Lord" (Joshua 24:15). Despite his churning emotions, at that moment he felt a deep peace in his heart. He felt sure that God was affirming him in the difficult choice he had made.

Edith

Edith's Amah bent down to peer anxiously into the little girl's open mouth before crowing in triumph.

"Yes, you did it, Mei Fuh!" she pronounced, in Chinese. "The rice is still there!"

Satisfied, Edith allowed her tongue to draw the rice out of her cheek, chewed it, and swallowed. Then a great beam spread over her childish features. This was a most important skill for her Chinese friends, learning how to drink tea down the right side of the mouth while keeping their rice intact in the left side. She had been practising it each time she visited their homes, and using chopsticks too, just like the little Chinese children sitting alongside her on the wooden bench.

Edith adored Chinese food. Her parents believed it was "too rich for little girls", but she had other ideas, and developed an uncanny knack of turning up at the homes of her Chinese neighbors just as they were serving their own meals. And she was never turned away. The sticky rice and flavoursome sauces were so much tastier than the bland scrambled eggs and toast her parents regarded as sensible food for young English children. Her mother didn't notice; she was busy working at the local girls' school in Wenzhou, teaching them about Jesus.

In fairness, Edith did her share of this too, despite her tender years. She would gather her Chinese playmates around her to play "church", and all the children knew who was in charge of proceedings. After they had sung a Christian chorus, she would ask, "Do you want to preach? No? Then I'll preach." "Do you want to pray? No? Then I'll pray!"

One day, unexpectedly, Edith received a lesson in prayer that she never forgot. Dr. Hoste was the director of the China Inland Mission, the mission agency her parents worked for, and he had allowed young Edith to accompany him on his daily prayer walk around the compound where they lived. Although she was aware of the great honor of this, nonetheless Edith couldn't keep herself from chattering away as they set out hand in hand across the veranda.

"You must stop talking now, Mei Fuh," Dr. Hoste told her after a few minutes, gently but firmly, so that she obeyed him at once. And then he began, in a heartfelt voice, to speak aloud to God, there and then as they walked together. Edith looked up at him, fascinated, as he prayed for all of the missionaries and their families by name, including herself, lifting need after need up to God. She had often heard her parents pray, and prayed with them, although this was done in their own home, and with eyes closed (and no peeking!). Now Edith began to realize that she could talk to God anywhere, anytime, and about anything. Later, listening to the grown-ups talk, she would realize that many of the prayers Dr. Hoste had prayed that day had been answered, and she was amazed.

These early lessons in faith stayed with young Edith, and when she looked back on her childhood she could never remember a time when she didn't believe in the Lord Jesus. But that didn't mean that she never had doubts.

One day, for instance, her mother read her the story of Jesus and Peter walking upon the water and she shook her head emphatically.

"I don't believe it. No one can walk on water!"

"Well, Mei Fuh," came the reply, "It's certainly true that no ordinary human being can walk on water. But what does that tell us about Jesus?"

After a few minutes of deep conversation, Edith realized that Jesus is God, and that God is the Creator, and can therefore do anything, even overriding the normal laws of creation to do miraculous things. And when she was convinced of something, Edith believed it fiercely. No doubt her Chinese friends received a powerful sermon that week!

When Edith's older sister Elsa came home from boarding school, one of the girls' favorite games to play was "Pilgrim's Progress". The classic book of that title by John Bunyan was beloved of many, including Edith and her sisters. It tells the story of the Christian life as a journey, a pilgrimage, in which the main character (aptly named "Christian") travels through many adventures to finally reach "The Celestial City". Edith loved to play act the first part of this famous story, where Christian is weighed down with a heavy burden until he is finally able to lay it down at the foot of the cross. The girls stuffed a pillowcase not only with the pillow but a few heavier objects for good measure, and then took turns climbing the stairs laboriously with this "burden" of sin slung over their backs. At the top of the staircase, they would bow at the foot of an imaginary cross and watch as the heavy burden of "sin" dropped from their hands and tumbled back down the stairs! It may have been just a game, but the significance of it was not lost on little Edith. Even if she didn't fully understand what sin was, she knew she was often naughty, and she knew there was forgiveness at the cross of Christ. The vivid imagery of Bunyan's book, and the game that reinforced it, contributed in no small part to her growing understanding of the Christian gospel.

Edith was the fourth child of George and Jessie Seville. She had two older sisters, Janet and Elsa, but tragically the couple's only son John had died when just a baby of eight months. This was not the first tragedy that had befallen Jessie, although Edith wasn't to find out about her mother's earlier losses until much later, when she was fourteen. On a rare evening alone, Edith's mother told her, to her astonishment, that she had in fact been married before.

"My first husband's name was Walter Greene," Jessie said, slowly. "He was a wonderful man, and I loved him very much. We were planning to go to China together."

This was back in 1894, and the China Inland Mission had been founded in 1865. Walter and Jessie had been reading and praying about Hudson Taylor's work, and both felt a strong call to follow in his footsteps. After they married, they began saving to go to Toronto Bible College to prepare for missionary work in China. Their first baby arrived at the end of that year, but heartbreakingly, he died at birth.

How Edith wept at this part of the story, and clung tightly to her mother! Yet more sadness was to come.

"And then, Edith, three weeks later Walter came home from his work burning with a fever. The doctor pronounced it "galloping consumption", a kind of tuberculosis which progressed very quickly and in those days had no cure."

Another three weeks later, after only a year of marriage, twenty-one-year-old Jessie Greene became a widow. Edith was stunned as she heard all this for the first time, and filled with grief for her mother's suffering. Yet she was even more full of admiration for her mother's courage and fortitude. For Jessie had not wavered from the course she and her young husband had set out upon. After his death, she continued to save her money. She went to the Prairie Bible Institute for three years of study to prepare her for the mission field. And in 1899, she sailed to Shanghai to serve with the China Inland Mission, just as she and Walter had planned.

Edith saw that her mother's suffering, though great indeed, had not shaken her faith, nor made her bitter. Though she had loved Walter dearly, and though she mourned deeply for him and the baby she had lost, the Lord Jesus was first in her heart. Despite these earthly losses, she pressed on to know Him, and to serve Him, and to share Him with others. Later, God had brought another young missionary into her life; Edith's father, George Seville. Initially, Jessie refused his advances, having decided never to remarry; but gradually, God changed her heart and she allowed herself to love again.

Before she was yet five years old, the time came for Edith and her family to leave China to return to the United States. As far as anyone knew, this would only be for a time of "furlough", perhaps a year at the most. It was explained to Edith that "furlough" is when missionaries return to their home countries for a few months to rest and to tell of the work which they have been doing. She was excited about visiting this new compound called America, full of relatives she had never met. She knew that these strangers would call her by her English name "Edith" instead of the Chinese name she had been so used to – "Mei Fuh" which meant "beautiful happiness". But much as she knew how important these relatives were to her parents, privately she was even more excited about the long boat trip to get there.

All the family's Chinese friends gathered to say goodbye before the old boat named "The China" set out from Shanghai to take them back to America. Yet in their sorrow at parting there was the happy expectation of a reunion to come, since the Seville family were expected to return in a few months for at least another seven years. Nobody knew then that this would be a permanent goodbye; for a year later, Jessie was refused the necessary medical approval to return to China.

Meanwhile, for little Edith, life in the U.S.A. was a culture shock that nothing could have prepared her for. There were plenty of thrilling new experiences – her first elevator ride, her first train ride, her first meetings with aunts and uncles and cousins in Ohio – and, of course, her first experience of an American school. Strangely, although it might have seemed natural for Edith to feel like an outsider in China, it was at school in California that she was really to know the uncomfortable feeling of being "different". During recess the other children would point at her and sing the mocking rhyme: "Chinky, chinky Chinaman, sitting on a fence; trying to make a dollar out of fifteen cents!" Edith refused to be intimidated, but, hands on hips, gave the indignant reply, "Well, they could as well! Which is more than could be said for you!" She always felt fiercely loyal to the country she had considered her home, and the people who lived there.

It was an unsettling time for Edith and her family, as they moved to four new "homes" in as many years. Amidst all the changes, Edith's Christian faith continued to grow and develop. It was in California, at the Baptist church the family attended, that Edith decided she wanted to be baptized, so that she could take communion and truly identify herself with the "family" of Christian believers. Although she was just seven years old, this was desperately important to her, so she was bold enough to ask if she could meet with the board of deacons. She sat across from these serious older men on a little chair, swinging her legs as they asked her a series of questions to assess her understanding of the Christian faith and what she was entering into.

"Do you believe that Jesus is God, Edith?"

"Oh yes!" the little girl replied, emphatically. "And he came into the world to die for us on the cross, to take the punishment for our sins."

It was the message Edith had always believed, and always would.

Two moves later, the family settled in Newburgh, New York, where Edith's father was to be the pastor of Westminster Independent Presbyterian Church. This was to be their home for the next seven years, and the place where Edith had her first real opportunity to defend her faith. Her best friend Emily was a Christian Scientist. She didn't believe that "matter" – material things – really existed; instead it was all about the mind. Edith and Emily would have long discussions about their different beliefs, often consulting a variety of books to support their arguments – not least, for Edith of course, the Bible! From these discussions, her own voracious reading, and listening to her parents' conversation, Edith grew in her confidence to speak about her Christian faith and to stand up for biblical truth when she heard it opposed.

Learning to defend her faith wasn't the only way that God was preparing Edith for her future ministry. She was also learning, from her mother, the domestic skills of managing a home on a very limited budget. Jessie had taught herself to sew with the help of a correspondence course, and soon developed a talent for creating marvellous items of clothing out of remnants of fabric she bought on sale. As George Seville's salary was small, Jessie learned to make the best of simple ingredients to serve her family tasty meals, attractively presented. These were skills Edith was able to imitate and develop, particularly after high school when she entered Beaver College to study Home Economics. This was actually a course that included a lot of academic study, particularly in the sciences and psychology, but alongside this was the practical study of many of the skills Edith believed would help her to be a good homemaker one day: food, interior decorating, dressmaking and so on. No doubt it might sound old-fashioned to some now, but to Edith this was simply good sense. She believed strongly in the value of "home", and saw it as a vital thing to invest time and effort into establishing. Yet she didn't find the idea of doing so dull or limiting, but instead saw it as something creative and exciting. She wanted to do what she had seen her mother do so many times over the last few years: to make each new house truly a "home", and to make a little go a long way. She could have had no idea, during her years at home and at Beaver, just how useful these skills were going to be; or how extensively God was going to use them.

Learning and Longing

The house on Ashmead Place South, to which Fran accompanied Edith that memorable evening in June 1932, had not been her family's home for long. Edith's high school years had involved yet more moving around, from Newburgh to Toronto, and then finally, for her final year of high school, back once more to Germantown. Her father was now working as the assistant editor for the monthly magazine of the China Inland Mission, "China's Millions". For Edith, this had meant the lonely experience of joining a senior class of young people who had been together for three years — and now with a Canadian accent that made her stand out even more.

Although she didn't yet know it, meeting Fran Schaeffer that night marked a new beginning in Edith's life. During her high school years, Edith had felt increasingly torn between two worlds. Although her Christian faith never faltered, she had none of the deep friendships she craved in which to discuss ideas and opinions. Her oldest sister Janet had fallen away from faith during her time at college, and the conversations the sisters had about it only strengthened Edith's resolve to keep learning enough to be able to defend her faith intellectually. On the other hand, she felt guilty for secretly enjoying some of the pleasures that Christians seemed to dismiss as "worldly", such as wearing nice clothes, and going to dances. Her parents had forbidden her to go to dances and movies, and she didn't feel good about deceiving them, but part of her just wanted to be "normal" and fit in.

So that Sunday night meeting was a pivotal moment for both Fran and Edith. Both of them had sorely felt the lack of good Christian friends their own age, and both dared to hope this new "friendship" might meet that need.

From the beginning, things moved quickly. Fran called on Edith, as promised, that Wednesday evening after work, and a couple of weeks later visited the family for the weekend at a missionary cottage in New Jersey where they were staying for a summer holiday. During that weekend Fran and Edith walked together the whole length of the Boardwalk to Atlantic City and back, seven miles in all, talking the whole way. There was so much to find out about one another! Yet in the midst of their discussion of books and ideas they didn't neglect to observe the beauty of God's creation, which seemed only heightened by being able to enjoy it together. Back home in Germantown, they spent much of that August together, going to concerts, to the movies and to the Philadelphia Museum of Art. Fran was also enjoying getting to know Edith's parents, especially over games of tennis with her father. Much as he loved his own parents, it was a joy to be able to share with George and Jessie Seville about the things that fired up his heart.

One evening just before Fran was due to return to college, he picked Edith up in the car and drove her sixty miles to a particularly beautiful spot where a bridge carried a canal over a river. As they quietly shared the moment together under the glow of a full moon, Fran plucked up the courage to lean over and kiss Edith under the rim of her big floppy hat. After a few moments of silence, he then got up rather abruptly to lead Edith back to the car. As he opened the passenger door for her, he awkwardly mumbled, "I'm sorry … I shouldn't have done that."

Edith felt rather crushed! She had no idea at the time how conflicted he was feeling. Since Fran had given his heart to Christ two years before, he had been completely focused on his plans. He was clear that Jesus came first in his heart. And now, the depth of his feelings for Edith had thrown him. What he admired most in her was the faith they shared, yet he was aware how easy it would be for her to rival Christ in his affections. That night, after dropping Edith off with perfect courtesy, he went home and wrote in his diary:

> *It would be an easy matter,*
> *To let my passions run riot.*
> *Easy that is, if it were not for Thee,*
> *Guiding us, keeping us strong.*
> *May we find our happiness in Thy way.*[1]

So Fran returned to college, but added writing regular letters to Edith to his already busy schedule of activities. He had thrown himself fully into life at Hampden-Sydney that first year. As well as studying hard, he had joined a fraternity, become a member of the Ministerial Association and was helping to run the Student Christian Association. He joined the Literary Society and took part in debates, and kept himself fit by being on the track team, even if he did later joke that "with a few rare exceptions I chased everyone else around the track!" He also began to teach at a Sunday school for black children at a local settlement, an act of service to God which he grew to love and would continue to do for the whole of his four years at college, becoming as involved as he could in the lives of those children and their families.

Fran was still a very new Christian when he went to college, and his faith had certainly been tested from the start. As it turned out, ministerial students were given a hard time. But after a miserable first few weeks on the Fourth Passage, Fran had begun to find his own ways of dealing with it.

"Hey Philly!"

---

1. Ibid, p. 135.

As Fran trudged wearily up the staircase to the Fourth Passage with his arms full of books, he froze at the sound of his roommate's voice. He looked up, and Snerp was leaning against the wall at the top of the steps, his thin face formed into an unpleasant sneer and his eyes glinting in anticipation.

"I saw ya, Philly," he said slowly, shaking his head in mock disapproval. "Outside without your cap on, again. Why, that's against the rules, Philly … you know that."

Fran knew what was coming. During those first few weeks he had been beaten by Snerp for countless instances of petty rule breaking, real or invented. It was a freshman's inevitable fate – they even had a name for it: "hazing". It was clear how much his roommate relished this unofficial responsibility to discipline him. But Fran's tolerance levels were wearing thin. He saw the familiar coat hanger in Snerp's big hands: his weapon of choice. Slowly, he continued to climb to the top of the stairs.

"Books down, Philly, and come over here," Snerp drawled.

There was the sound of a door opening, and Fran saw Pat, the "top dog" of the fourth passageway, emerge from his room and pause in the doorway to watch the forthcoming entertainment. Suddenly Fran decided enough was enough. He lunged towards Snerp, catching him off guard and sending both of them tumbling to the ground. After several minutes of wrestling, Fran gained the upper hand and found himself on top of his roommate, with Snerp at his mercy. For a moment they both paused, glaring at one another as they panted to catch their breath.

There was an amused chuckle behind them and Pat stepped forward, holding out his hand to Fran.

"Hey," he said, grinning, as Fran took his hand and hauled himself up off the floor, leaving Snerp red-faced and sullen. "You're the biggest little man I've ever seen, Philly."

That was the end of Fran's hazing. It certainly wasn't his intended way of dealing with things, but having earned his neighbors' grudging respect, he soon set up a Fourth Passageway "Prayer Meeting". The meetings were short and simple, as everyone was very busy and Fran wanted to make it as easy as possible for people to come. He would read a passage of the Bible, say one or two things about it and then allow others the chance to pray aloud before doing so himself. It was a small group, but it slowly grew.

Fran was very persistent in inviting the non-attenders, which they didn't always appreciate. One day he stood outside his neighbor Chisel's door, took a breath and knocked. Not getting an answer, he opened the door.

"What d'you want, Philly?" Chisel looked as if he had just got back from the gym; freshly showered, worn out and clearly not in the mood to be pestered. The warning tone in his voice didn't deter Fran.

"How about coming to prayer meeting?" he asked.

It was one too many invitations for Chisel. Without missing a beat, he pulled a can of talcum powder from his gym bag, and threw it across the room at Fran, hitting him just above the eye. For a long moment, they both stayed glued to the spot, as blood began seeping from the gash on Fran's face.

"So ... are you coming to prayer meeting?" he asked again.

Chisel shook his head in disbelief. "Look, Philly, tell you what. If you want me to come, I'll come ... if you can carry me there."

So Fran marched across the room, blood still dripping down his face. Chisel was a good six feet two inches to Fran's modest five-six, but nonetheless the smaller man hoisted Chisel over his shoulder in a fireman's lift and staggered with his heavy load out of the room, along the corridor and down the stairs to the meeting.

Fran also had an unusual way of getting his college neighbors along to church with him on Sunday mornings. Despite it being the time of "Prohibition" (when drinking alcohol was made illegal in the U.S.), nonetheless the students found ways and means of getting their hands on a fair amount of alcohol, particularly on Saturday nights. When they came home drunk and unable to grope their way up to their rooms in the darkened halls and stairwells, they soon began to call for "Philly ... !" Knowing he would be disturbed anyway, Fran began to stay up late on Saturday nights, appreciating the extra time to study. He would willingly go down to each drunken student who called for his help, guide him to his room, help him undress and get to bed, or under a cold shower if necessary! But there was one condition: "If I look after you when you come home late on a Saturday night, you have to come to church with me the next morning!" So it was not uncommon to see Fran head off to church with several large athletes stumbling along behind him, looking rather the worse for wear!

By the end of that first year, Fran was truly accepted and even admired by the other students on the Fourth Passage, even those who had no interest in spiritual things. He certainly didn't fit their stereotype of what a ministerial student would be like. Unknowingly, Fran had developed an approach that would characterise his future ministry: engaging with the culture around him while being distinctive from it. He didn't earn his neighbors respect by standing in judgement on them, but by loving them, even as he refused to conform to their way of living. He had found that this was the best starting point for making the truth known to those around him.

Together or Apart?

"Well, I wish someone would tell me what this is all about!" remarked George Seville, Edith's father, shaking his head in bewilderment as he regarded his youngest daughter across the table. Edith wasn't prone to outbursts of emotion, but that evening there was no disguising the blotchy tear-stained face or lack of appetite as she stared miserably into her tomato soup. Her mother Jessie leaned over and gently patted Edith's shoulder, knowing that no words could heal her broken heart.

Fran and Edith had been faithful correspondents since August, writing to one another first twice, and then three times a week! No promises had been made, and the nature of their relationship had not yet been precisely defined. Edith only knew that she looked forward to Fran's letters more and more, and found herself sharing her own thoughts and ideas with increasing openness and familiarity. How she had looked forward to seeing him again, when he returned for his Christmas vacation! And now ... this.

It was New Year's Eve, and that afternoon as they walked together, Fran had abruptly announced his decision to end their correspondence and the growing relationship between them.

"I think I'm getting too fond of you, Edith," he explained regretfully. "And I'm not sure there is a future for us, together. I don't know where God is calling me yet, but I feel it might be somewhere I would need to go alone. Without a wife."

Edith tried hard not to betray her surprise and disappointment.

"I promise I'll continue to pray for you," he continued, earnestly. "And I hope you might agree to do the same for me."

"Of course," she answered, quickly, trying to smile.

It wasn't until she reached the safe haven of home that the tears began to flow. She did admire Fran's commitment to the Lord, and in some ways loved him all the better for it; but on the other hand, she wasn't sure he was right. If the Lord really was calling him to singleness on the mission field then … well, so be it. But Edith longed to serve God too, wherever He might lead her. She thought of her parents' happy marriage and faithful service together, and struggled to think of anywhere Fran might need to go where she could not and would not gladly follow.

After that quiet, awkward dinner, the telephone rang with a social invitation from friends. Determined not to wallow, Edith agreed to see in the New Year in one of their homes, listening to records. She felt heavy-hearted but had no desire to be alone that evening. However, as she was getting ready to go, the telephone rang again.

"It's me," said Fran, sounding utterly miserable. "I can't do it, Edith, I don't want to carry on without you. Can I come over?"

As relief flooded through her, Edith caught sight of the hallway clock and couldn't help but smile to herself. It had been just two hours since they had said their "forever" good-byes.

That night, Fran asked Edith if she would "wait" for him until they had both finished college. Although no formal marriage proposal was made, from that time on both Fran and Edith regarded themselves as engaged.

Even so, this wasn't to be the last time Fran felt challenged to surrender his relationship with Edith, if God desired it. During his final year at college two years later, when their now daily letters were increasingly concerned with plans for their future together, Fran felt the same conflict of heart as he listened to a hard-hitting talk by Dr. Howard Taylor, the son of Hudson Taylor, who had founded the China Inland Mission. Following the meeting, Fran committed his life to God afresh, feeling that he must be prepared to give up all for Christ. He promptly wrote to tell Edith of this experience, asking her directly if she felt the same way. Was she prepared even to surrender their future together, if that was what God required?

After a time of praying and soul-searching (with a few tears!), Edith penned her reply:

All my life since I have been tiny I have wanted His will for my life ... Yet as I've prayed for His will saying I would be willing to go anywhere – to the ends of the earth – I have also asked that He would give me a helpmate. When I loved and was loved by one who had the same purpose in life, I thought it was a direct answer to this prayer, and I really never faced the question of giving you up.

And now Franz, I cannot say that I feel any definite call to work alone – my heart and mind are open – but I still feel God has brought us together – that He has given us this good thing. God is a loving Father and His goodness is wonderful. I feel He can use us together to glorify His Kingdom ... But if you ever feel definitely called to work alone, know – that I have left our love in His hands. God doesn't have two right ways for us – if He did bring us together – if He does mean us to marry – then – He has a work for us, that can only be done together.

I love you
Edith[1]

Having confronted again this need to be sure that they were putting God first, Fran and Edith continued to move forward in faith together.

---

1. Ibid, p. 156.

* * *

"What are all those white rolls with ribbon around them?" Frank Schaeffer whispered. He was sitting beside the elegant young lady who was soon to be his daughter-in-law, feeling more than a little out of place in the grand chapel building and uncomfortably dressed up in his smart suit and tie.

"Those are the diplomas, Pop," Edith explained, gently. "Each graduate gets one, as proof of their B.A."

Frank had another question. He'd found his son's name in the programme but didn't understand the strange words beside it.

"Fran's got three words next to his name but some have only got two. That's good, isn't it?"

Edith nodded, with a warm smile. But she noticed a few disapproving looks from people sitting around them, so was careful to lean in even closer to reply.

"Yes, Pop," she whispered, right into his ear. "Fran's graduating *magna cum laude*, which means 'with great distinction'."

Frank gave her hand an answering squeeze, his chest swelling with pride. He still didn't fully understand Fran's changed ambitions, and had missed his son dearly over the past four years. But there was no denying the boy had worked hard! He felt a peculiar satisfaction in the fact that his son had more than held his own amongst these other young men, many of them from backgrounds of wealth and privilege.

The names were read out one by one, and each student ascended the platform to receive their diploma to furious applause. Once each one held their hard-earned roll of white parchment, it was time for special awards and prizes to be announced. And suddenly –

"Francis August Schaeffer!"

Frank and Edith clasped hands again as Fran stepped forward to be presented with a copper framed plaque.

The college president was smiling broadly. "This is awarded to the most outstanding Christian on campus during his four years."

Once the excitement of graduation was over, the next three weeks were filled with frantic wedding preparations. Needing all the extra income they could get, Fran came straight home and back to work at a bakery, college graduate or not! This would earn the couple their wedding cake, and a little more. Meanwhile, Edith and her mother worked busily on the dresses for the big day. Cotton dimity with pink and blue roses for Edith's sisters, the bridesmaids. Traditional white for Edith, who had made her own wedding gown as her last dressmaking project at college, and now had only to add the special finishing touches to make it perfect.

Aside from the preparations for the wedding day itself, Fran and Edith were gathering bits and pieces together to furnish the tiny apartment they had found to rent in central Philadelphia. They certainly couldn't afford new things, but both families passed on one or two items of furniture from their homes, such as the old bed and chest of drawers from Fran's childhood bedroom, which he sanded down and freshened up with a lick of paint. Other than that, they improvised and adapted whatever they could find, even making use of a set of springs from an old couch Fran found dumped behind a garage!

At last, the big day arrived. Edith was busy up until the very last moment when the cars arrived, arranging the bouquets and a wreath of white rosebuds for her hair. There was no time for deep romantic thoughts, not until she found herself being walked up the aisle to the rich, full notes of the organ. Her eyes scanned the church, delighted by the wild flowers their friends had used to decorate it and thrilled to see so many of the people she loved dressed up in their finery. She felt a burst of grateful relief to see that even Fran's mother, who'd been threatening not to come, had changed her mind and decided to attend the wedding after all! And then finally her eyes lifted shyly to Fran, standing at the front of the church, and looking at her just as though no one else was there at all.

For Better and for Worse

"Young man, have you any faults?" Edith had written adoringly to Fran during their courtship ... "No matter how much I pucker my brow – nary a one can I conjure up – It wouldn't make any difference if you did have – but you don't."

"You are what I could sit down and figure out that I wanted in a woman," Fran commented, in his turn. "But, how in the world, you, so gloriously perfect for a Christian's wife, have come to me I do not understand."[1]

This mutual delight in one another was wonderfully romantic, but it was not long into their married lives together before Fran and Edith were forced to confront some of the inevitable weaknesses in each one's characters. They both understood that as Christians, they were forgiven sinners being made into Christ's likeness, but that this was a work-in-progress that would continue throughout their earthly lives. As Edith later wrote, the grand promises they stood up to make that summer's day in 1935 were vows "for

---

1. Ibid, p. 147, p. 172.

imperfect people to make to imperfect people". She also described the vow to stick together "for better and for worse" as "a fantastically realistic promise"!

The "worse" that began on the couple's honeymoon was perhaps not so very bad, but certain things did happen to rather tarnish the fairy tale for Edith. As they departed through the crowd of guests throwing rice, Edith proudly wore the special white "going away" suit she had made for the occasion. Hot and weary, the couple stopped on the outskirts of town to have a drink at a drugstore, but Edith had failed to notice that a previous customer had spilt chocolate milkshake all over her stool. The skirt of her suit was ruined! All those hours of careful sewing – wasted!

She tried very hard to bite her tongue and not make a fuss, as Fran consoled her and reminded her that this special time of starting their lives together was far more important than any skirt. But the following day, looking around at the poky cabin they had rented overnight for $1.50, the tears of homesickness began to flow. Determined not to spend much money, Fran and Edith had rented the cheap cabin and brought all their groceries with them, not really thinking about the practicalities of the soaring temperatures and the tiny space. Now the cabin reeked of cabbage, and the little jar of butter Edith brought had melted into liquid fat. Edith could almost have laughed, through her tears, as she looked at her dainty clothes and satin nightgown, so thoughtfully handmade and packed. It wasn't quite the perfect fairy tale she had imagined! But perhaps it was a good lesson learned. Although Fran and Edith were always to be thrifty people who managed to do a lot with a little, they would later urge newly married couples to try to budget for at least "a few days of special luxury" on their honeymoon, that important time of starting married life together.

When the honeymoon was over, the new Mr. and Mrs. Schaeffer spent the whole summer helping at a Christian camp near Lake Michigan, before driving back to Philadelphia in time for Fran to start seminary in the Fall, in preparation for being ordained as a Presbyterian minister. Since the Saturday night traffic was slow and Edith had passed her driving test, Fran was willing to let her take her turn behind the wheel. Feeling bored in the crawling traffic, Edith glimpsed a pretty fountain out of the window and exclaimed to Fran.

"Look, Fran! See that lovely fountain!"

At that moment there was an alarming crunch: distracted, Edith had managed to drive into the bumper of the car in front. Fran jumped out of the car to deal with the situation while Edith waited, shaken and anxious in the driver's seat. She was dismayed when Fran returned, only to yell at her for being such an idiot! Hoping to be forgiven for her mistake, instead Edith found herself on the receiving end of a tirade of harsh, critical words.

When he had finished letting off steam, Edith exhaled slowly, looking straight ahead away from him. "Well then. That's it. I'm never driving again."

And she never did. For if Fran struggled with a quick temper, Edith in her turn could be stubborn.

These early conflicts in their relationship were unpleasant, but not really surprising. Fran and Edith were, after all, two very different characters coming together to embark on a new stage of life and having to learn to adapt to one another's ways of doing things. Thankfully, on the other side of it, there were plenty of consolations in their married life.

While Fran began his three years of study at Westminster Theological Seminary, to become a pastor, Edith supported them both by putting her practical skills to good use as a seamstress and leather worker. She worked hard to design, make and sell clothes and leather belts, which brought in just enough money for them to live on while Fran studied. In the evenings, while Fran pored over his books, Edith stayed up with him late into the night, sewing. Fran would very often break into the productive silence with, "Hey, do you know what McRae said today?" and a long discussion of theological ideas would begin. Edith treasured those times, because it helped her too to develop her thinking and benefit from the seminary education Fran was getting.

When Fran went off to college each day, he took with him a packed lunch Edith had carefully prepared.

Even though she wasn't leaving the apartment, she liked to make herself exactly the same packed lunch he would be having, so that it felt like they were together, sharing the same experience! It helped her to keep thinking of him, and praying for him during the day. The apartment they shared was certainly small, but they had worked hard to make the space into a home. They were particularly grateful that the kitchen opened out onto an area of tin roof that came to function as their "garden" when they filled pots with seeds that would soon flower into a beautiful crop of petunias, ivy and blue morning glories. They cherished that little outdoor space and the daily dose of sunshine it afforded them – even if nothing could be done about the view of untended backyards and ugly buildings!

Although they settled down as much as they could during the two years in that first home together, Fran and Edith were very aware that this was a transitional time in their lives, a time of preparation for whatever God had in store for them in the future. Beside the little table in the kitchen where they ate their meals, they put up a world map and beside it a map of China that Dr. Howard Taylor had signed, and upon which Fran had written: "Serve the Lord with gladness." As they prayed to thank God for their food, they often prayed about their future together, open to going wherever on those maps God might send them. They made the most of Sundays to spend time with both of their families, rightly anticipating that this time of living near to their parents might not last.

Two exciting things happened soon after Fran and Edith's first wedding anniversary. Edith discovered that she was expecting their first child, and Fran had to be admitted to hospital for an emergency operation to have his appendix removed. The hospital stay lasted two weeks, and Edith brought him study notes she had carefully copied out from his friends, so that he could keep up his work. Meanwhile, poor Edith, in the throes of morning sickness, would make daily visits to the ladies' toilet on her way to and from the hospital cafeteria!

The Schaeffers learned a valuable lesson about prayer through this experience, one that would stand them in good stead throughout their ministry. When Fran was almost due to leave, they were confronted with a hospital bill that would cost all the money they had saved to pay for their baby's birth, which would also require a hospital stay. After much prayer, Edith went nervously to see the hospital administrators and explain their situation. The sombre man behind the desk listened quietly.

"Well, there is a fund to help those in financial need," he explained, when she had finished speaking. "However, it is administered on a month by month basis, and it rather depends on what is left in the account for this month. I'll tell you what, why don't you come back and see me again tomorrow, and I will find out for you. But I can't promise anything – it may be that the money for this month has been used by now."

The next day, Edith went back for the verdict, anxious and yet trying hard to trust in the Lord to provide. To her amazement, the man told her that there was seventy-five dollars left in that month's account – the exact total on the hospital bill Edith had clasped in her hand! The Lord had indeed provided, and in such a way that they could not doubt it was His doing.

This confirmation that God was a personal God, who delighted in having his children come to him for help, was in contrast to the views of some of the professors and their wives at Westminster at that time. Indeed, at a wives' prayer meeting, Edith had once found herself reprimanded for praying something too specific. The professor's wife told Edith sternly that since God is Sovereign, we should only pray for His will to be done, which should not include any material requests, only spiritual things. Edith felt they were saying that God didn't want to be "bothered" by their little problems and needs. That differed strongly from the faith she had experienced within the China Inland Mission and in the lives of her parents. Now this answer to their prayers for help was a loving reminder that God did care, and did want to be "bothered" with their requests!

Those different ideas about prayer that Edith had encountered reflected a growing conflict within the Presbyterian Church at that time, not only about the

nature of God but also about how to interpret the Bible.
In 1929, Dr. Gresham Machen, a hero of the Schaeffers,
had founded Westminster out of growing concern over
the "modernist" theology which was being promoted
at Princeton. He was well-known for his high view
of Scripture as being the literal and inerrant word of
God, meaning that it contains no errors or mistakes.
However, after his death in 1937, new divisions sprung
up at Westminster. While the college still stood firmly
upon the truth of the Bible, there were two main
issues upon which people disagreed. The first was on
Christian liberty, particularly in the area of drinking
alcohol. While some argued in favor of a Christian's
freedom in such matters, others felt that Christians
should abstain from drinking. It is worth remembering
that the Prohibition, the time when there was a
nationwide ban on the consumption of alcohol, had
only ended four years previously in 1933, so this was a
relatively new issue for Christians to deal with. At that
time, Fran chose to side with his professor, Dr. McRae,
who was against Christians drinking alcohol.

The second issue was concerning prophecy,
particularly disagreement about how to interpret
some of the Bible's prophecies about the "end times"
in the book of Revelation. These differences eventually
resulted in another major split, and the formation of
a new college in Wilmington, Delaware, where Fran
would transfer for his final year of study. It was a painful
upheaval, but one which Fran and Edith believed to

be necessary at the time. Looking back in later years, they came to regret some of the words that had been spoken on both sides, and apologized to many of the men concerned. Edith wisely realized that the strong or harsh words spoken during such disagreements can cast a longer shadow than the "issues" themselves.

Once resigned to the necessity of the split, Fran and Edith became heavily involved in setting up the new college and making it ready for the influx of new students who would be arriving ... and all this the same summer that they welcomed their first child, baby Priscilla, into the world! In those days, it was normal for a mother and newborn baby to stay in the hospital for two weeks, with visiting hours in the afternoon and evening. Fran was frantically busy helping Dr. McRae organise all the details for the new seminary, so Edith was careful to keep the final hour between eight and nine free of other visitors so that she and her husband could share that time together. Alas, many were the evenings when she would wait in vain for those visits, only to have him rush in, full of apologies, at five minutes to nine! Sometimes she fought back tears and resentful words, but in her heart she knew it wasn't Fran's fault. Fran was busy doing the work he had been given to do, and the new seminary was a project they both believed in wholeheartedly.

A month later, she left Priscilla in her mother's care for the day to go to Wilmington with Fran in search of suitable accommodation for the new students. Once this had been found, Fran was also given the task of preparing the houses on a meagre budget, finding toilets and other fittings in junk yards, organizing plumbers and electricians, hunting down second-hand furniture and everything else that needed to be done in readiness for the start of the first term. Edith was also hard at work sewing curtains and slipcovers for the student lounge as well as their own new home. It was a whirlwind of a summer.

Finally, the hard work was completed and Faith Theological Seminary was open for business. Fran was the first "official" student to register, and nine months later the first to graduate and be ordained in the Bible Presbyterian Church. Fran and Edith had mixed feelings about moving on. It had been a strange year in many ways, but a special one nonetheless. Since Fran had persuaded Edith's father to join the faculty of the new seminary, it had also been a time of living and serving alongside George and Jessie Seville, in a way that would never be repeated. Edith knew she would miss them dearly, and yet both she and Fran were excited about the future that lay ahead of them. At Fran's seminary graduation, they sang the rousing hymn: "Give Tongues of Fire to Preach Thy Word", and Edith felt her heart soar with emotion. Silently she prayed, "Please, Lord, give Fran a tongue of fire to preach your Word. Never let the fire cool off."

Ministry in America

At the end of Matthew's gospel, before Jesus ascended into heaven, He spoke these well-known words to his disciples, often referred to as "The Great Commission": "Go and make disciples of all nations, baptizing them in the name of the Father and of the Son and of the Holy Spirit, and teaching them to obey everything I have commanded you" (Matthew 28:18-20, NIV). As disciples of Jesus in the twentieth century, Fran and Edith had both made this their life's objective: to obey Jesus and make His name known by teaching others about Him. It was their desire both as individuals, and now as a married couple and a family.

With the example of Edith's parents, and her happy childhood memories of China, it was very natural that their thoughts had instinctively turned to missionary work overseas. Although Fran had no real experience of this kind of service, it was something that excited him too, particularly as he had listened to inspiring addresses over the years by various missionaries such as Dr. Howard Taylor of the CIM. Yet as Fran's ordination had drawn near, the Lord's leading seemed to be, for now, towards ministry at home in the United States. As they packed to move again, it was not without a pang of sadness that they took down the world map from their wall. Here they were, heading back to the state of Pennsylvania! Fran was going to be the pastor of a church in Grove City; 350 miles away, but hardly the other side of the world. Still, they knew that God could use them to further His kingdom wherever He chose to send them, and that their own countrymen needed the gospel as much as anyone. So they threw themselves whole-heartedly into this new ministry.

When they arrived in Grove City, the Covenant Presbyterian Church consisted of only eighteen adults, who had left the main Presbyterian Church because of its increasingly liberal, unbiblical teaching and had started meeting in a nearby hall. These few didn't even bring their own children along, because they wanted them to be part of the larger Sunday school at the church they'd left – so the first Sunday morning Edith felt very conspicuous trying to quietly occupy one-year-old Priscilla while her husband – the "Reverend Schaeffer"! – preached his first sermon. Despite the distraction of caring for her daughter, she tried to keep praying throughout Fran's talk, asking God to speak through him and touch the hearts of those who heard his message. This was to be a habit Edith continued throughout Fran's ministry, whenever she had the chance. She also prayed that they themselves would let

God speak to them through His Word. She knew only too well that she and Fran were not on some kind of separate, "super-human" level above those who listened to him preach – they needed God's Spirit just as much to help them to grow and change, wherever change was needed.

The first thing Fran wanted to do, in his new role, was to reach out to children in the town, and try to begin a proper children's ministry at the new church. Having been a boy himself, he decided that the best way to appeal to the local boys was through their stomachs! He found the perfect spot in Grove City park to host a "hot dog roast" and then drove around the town inviting along all the boys he met out playing, until his Ford was packed to bursting with children, inside and out. Needless to say, this is not a method of evangelism that would be recommended today! But it worked. When the boys were well fed and games had been played, Fran spoke about the God who had created the world, and they listened to "Rev" with genuine interest. There were several of these hot dog roasts before the Schaeffers and their new church family began to plan their first "Summer Bible School". The boys Fran had been getting to know through the hot dog roasts served as a mini outreach team, taking Fran around town to meet their friends and hand out leaflets to their parents. Sometimes this even led to "Rev" being invited into their homes and given the opportunity to really talk about the Christian faith. Although Edith and the other volunteers were apprehensive as they waited outside the church hall that first morning of Bible School, to their amazement seventy-nine children turned up! By the end of the week, they had a hundred.

Under Fran's ministry, the little church slowly grew. By the time the Schaeffers had been there three years, the congregation had grown to 110 members, and new people were coming to the services each week. They had outgrown the hall, and moved into a new church building the members had constructed themselves, with Fran taking an active role; even helping to paint the steeple when he was one of the only men prepared to climb the ladder high enough! It was second nature to Fran after years of scampering up and down ladders without a thought as a boy, helping his Pop.

In fact, it was during this time in Grove City that God broke into Pop's life in a dramatic fashion. Bessie telephoned her son one day to say that Frank had suffered a stroke and that he must come at once. Fran did so, and when he walked into his father's bedroom was greeted with the words he'd prayed for years to hear: "Boy, tell me about that Jesus of yours." That very day, his father became his brother in Christ! Soon afterwards, Fran's parents came to stay with him and Edith for an extended time as Frank recovered. It certainly added to Edith's workload, which already included hosting meetings in their home, housework, dressmaking, Sunday school teaching and the care of little Priscilla, on top of the extra tiredness of a new pregnancy! However, in gratitude, Grandfather Schaeffer contributed greatly to their busy household with the substantial gifts of a first washing machine and an electric refrigerator – appliances that were to make a huge difference to Edith's daily work.

Although the ministry at Covenant Presbyterian Church was growing and thriving, an opportunity arose for Fran to come and preach as a "candidate" in Chester, Pennsylvania. He might not have taken it but for a comment from one of the elders in Grove City, who expressed his opinion that three years was about the time when a minister would have said all that he had to say and should go and say it somewhere else! Fran was offered the position in Chester, at a church of around five hundred, where he would be the Associate Pastor under Dr. Lathem, whom he knew from serving on the Summer Bible School Association. So the family moved once more; a family of four now, for they had joyfully welcomed baby Susan into the world earlier that summer.

Chester was a much larger place than Grove City, with a more diverse population. As well as preaching on a Sunday evening, Fran had many opportunities to talk to a range of people about Jesus, from laborers and truck drivers to students, professors and businessmen. Being from a working class, or "blue collar" background himself, Fran was down to earth and able to speak to people on their own terms. Yet he was also a deep thinker and philosopher, who would, years later, be described as "the missionary to intellectuals"! In other words, he could talk to anyone.

Fran also saw people as individuals, and genuinely cared about their needs. In Grove City, he had already established the habit of regularly visiting people in their homes. Continuing this practice in Chester, he got to know Ralphie and his family. Ralphie was a young boy with Down's Syndrome, whose parents could not afford to give him the special education he needed. Although Fran had no particular knowledge or expertise in this area, he began to visit Ralphie twice a week to teach him what he could, using props such as colorful blocks in all different shapes. Later, another girl with similar needs joined the "class". It was perhaps an unusual way for a pastor to spend his time, but it really mattered to Fran and felt as important to him as any aspect of his ministry.

During their time in Chester, there was also another building project for Fran to assist with. Because of his practical know-how, he was the one assigned to work with the contractor on all the plans, making use of the mechanical drawing he had studied in high school as well as his building experience.

However, one of the highlights of the Chester years was a ministry that took the Schaeffer family away from the church itself, as they took a group of young people of all ages into the Blue Ridge Mountains of Virginia for a Summer Camp. They had already fallen in love with the mountains the previous summer when they had helped run a Bible camp in New England. Now they were excited about getting out of the city once more, and teaching young people Bible truths in such a beautiful, natural setting. Plans had been carefully made, speakers and leaders lined up, and campers signed up ... but there was one problem. At the last minute, the experienced man whom Fran had found to cook for the camp had to pull out. It presented a real difficulty, especially at this late stage. There were 118 people who needed feeding, and while several church ladies had been lined up to help, it was something quite different to take charge of it all – the menus, the shopping, the organizing of a team.

"Don't worry!" Edith said, confidently. "I can do it! I can just multiply up the recipes we use at home."

She rose to the challenge. The years of learning cooking from her mother, and at college, had no doubt helped to prepare her, even if she had never taken on a catering project on this scale before. She also knew that many of the children who came on the camp didn't have the benefit of a good diet at home, and she relished the opportunity to feed them up with fresh fruit and vegetables, and balanced, healthy meals. With this in mind, she even managed to stretch the food budget to include a daily vitamin tablet for each child!

Meanwhile, Fran, as camp leader, was in his element; teaching the boys from the front but also getting alongside them, talking to them, playing with them, hiking with them. When Fran and Edith later reflected on the success of the camp – the many young people who had said that they never wanted to go home, but wished they could stay forever – they pondered this mix of spiritual food, good physical food and the beautiful environment, all of which had contributed to making the experience so special for everyone. They also realized that it was partly the homey, family atmosphere that had been created by having "Rev" up front, his wife in the kitchen, and their two little girls running around underfoot! Many of these elements would continue to be vital parts of their future ministry.

It was after this camp, in the autumn of 1942, that the effects of the U.S. involvement in the Second World War began to be felt more keenly. Air raid practices took place regularly, which meant enforced blackouts for the whole town. As a pastor, Fran was allowed to keep driving even after the sirens sounded, with his headlights painted in black except for a thin slit in the middle to see by. Inside, people were not allowed any lights on unless their blackout equipment – black plastic on the windows, or blankets or whatever they could find – was good enough. It wasn't an easy winter for the Schaeffer family, especially as both Priscilla and Susan went through a prolonged period of illness, getting chicken pox, whooping cough and then mumps, one after the other! Edith would rush to little Susan during her worst coughing fits and carry her to the hall, where the blackout curtains on the stairwell made it possible to turn a light on. There she would rock her and nurse her, feeding her little sips of orange juice which would then be thrown up during the next bout of coughing!

It was during another blackout, in the early summer of 1943, that Pop finally breathed his last, three days after suffering a second stroke. This time, Fran and Edith had the comfort of knowing that his future with the Lord was secure. They sat by his bedside, reading the Bible to him and talking to him; even though he never regained consciousness, it seemed that the faintest trace of a smile would cross his face. When he died, at three in the morning during a blackout, they were comforted by the promises about heaven at the end of the Bible: "The city does not need the sun or the moon to shine on it, for the glory of God gives it light, and the Lamb is its lamp. The nations will walk by its light ... there will be no night there" (Revelation 21: 23-25 NIV).

The decision to move again, when Fran received a "call" to the Bible Presbyterian Church in St. Louis, was not an easy one for the Schaeffers. They were leaving behind many people whom they had grown to love. But over some weeks, as Fran prayed about it, he felt increasingly sure that the Lord was leading him to take this opportunity. Edith was less certain.

One day, as the move drew closer, Edith was left at home while Fran paid more of the "farewell" visits he had pledged to make to each family in the church. Unexpectedly, an older lady in the church came to see Edith and tried to persuade her that the family should stay. When she left, Edith found herself down on her knees, burying her tear-stained face in the cushion of the armchair as she prayed.

"Oh Lord, I don't even know how to pray ... but how can we be sure that we are right? What about all these people? Please, please make your will clear."

The unexpected answer came in words to a hymn that sprang to Edith's mind. She began to sing them aloud, to the familiar tune of an old favorite by Frances Havergal:

> *My will made known to thee,*
> *As thou dost wait on me.*
> *The future now thou canst not see*
> *But I will work for thee.*
> *My will, My will made known to thee,*
> *As thou dost wait on me.*
> *My will, my will made known to thee,*
> *As thou dost wait on me.*[1]

Later, when she looked up the hymn, Edith found that it had no such verse! She knew that the Lord had put these words in her heart, and with them a new peace. She was confident that God would keep them on the right path and make the way clear, as long as they kept "waiting" on him, through prayer and obedience. Often in the future, when the family faced similar times of uncertainty, Edith would find comfort in these words.

---

1. Ibid, p. 225.

To St. Louis and Beyond

"Now, girls, let's sit down over here a minute, on this bench."

Obediently, Priscilla and Susan sat, the latter swinging her short legs in eager anticipation.

"Take your time, girls. I want you to look, really look, at all the paintings," said Fran, with a tone of something almost like reverence in his voice. Ever since his very first visit to the Museum of Art in Philadelphia all those years ago, Fran had been fascinated by art of all kinds. It was a passion he was determined to pass on to his children, particularly as it was something he felt he had missed out on for so much of his life. "Take a good, long look. And then tell me which picture you like best, and why."

"That one! That one!" three-year-old Susan sang out, joyfully, earning herself a stern 'shhhh!' from her older sister.

Her father gave her an encouraging smile. "That one is lovely, Susan. How about you, Priscilla? Which one would you like to hang on your bedroom wall, if you could?"

The girls sat quietly for a few minutes, letting their eyes rove slowly around the large room, from one painting to the next. They loved this special time with their father on his day off, especially these trips to his favorite place of all, the St. Louis Art Museum.

Once he had drawn from them their thoughts and ideas about the pictures in the room, Fran told them a little about the history of some of them, before unpacking the bag of art materials they had brought with them. There was good quality art paper and pencils, crayons and charcoal. They passed another happy hour or so making sketches of their favorite pictures, as well as drawing a few inspired creations of their own. And even if the results of Susan's artistic endeavors were of a different level of maturity to seven-year-old Priscilla's, one would never know it from their father's delight in both.

The Schaeffers loved bustling, metropolitan St. Louis, with its museum, its zoo, its enormous Forest Park. The concerts, the shops and restaurants, fine schools and two universities … it was all on a different scale to anywhere they had lived before. They loved the large, three-story house they had found to live in, close enough to the zoo that they could sometimes hear the roar of the lions at night. Most of all, they loved their growing ministry in the heart of the city – even if the responsibilities and the packed schedule of meetings sometimes left Fran with little time for family life.

Once again, Edith threw herself into the ministry at her husband's side. Together they worked particularly hard on building up a children's ministry that eventually developed further than either of them had planned or anticipated.

Edith began by inviting local friends of Priscilla and Susan to a Bible class she led in their own basement. There were children there from a variety of families, Lutheran or Catholic, Jewish or of no religious background at all. Edith taught them stories from the Bible using colorful felt pictures and props, taught them to pray and played games with them. There were always fun activities to do, not to mention home-baked cookies and other goodies. At the same time, Fran began to invite a group of church women to the Parsonage each week, so that he and Edith could model how to teach such a class to children. These ladies in turn set up groups in their own homes, and together they would all meet up each week to share notes, prepare resources and pray for the children who came.

It began simply as a way for the church to reach out to the children of St. Louis, but Fran and Edith's model was so successful that it began to be used in other churches and even in other denominations further afield. Eventually, this grew into a work called "Children for Christ", and the Schaeffers had a whole new sphere of ministry opening up before them.

Meanwhile, Fran had become involved with the Independent Board of Presbyterian Foreign Missions, an organization that Dr. Machen had set up before his death. When the war came to an end in 1945, the aftermath for the war-torn countries in Europe was very much on everybody's minds. Fran was particularly concerned about the effect that liberal theology might be having on the churches there.

At a meeting of the board in 1947, Fran spoke up.

"It seems to me that we should find out just what the situation is in the churches. So many have been isolated in those countries during the war – isolated from the new sweep of danger, theologically – and are sending their theological students to study in America without any knowledge of what is being taught. We also ought to find out how children can be given Bible teaching, apart from the churches – something like the "Children for Christ' work."[1]

After much discussion, a conclusion was reached. Yes, they agreed that someone should go on a thorough tour of Europe and report back. And that person should be Fran Schaeffer.

So that summer, Fran set out on a three-month tour of Europe, with a packed itinerary of church visits and interviews. He would travel by air, by sea and by train, sleeping in fifty-three different places in thirteen different countries!

This also involved some upheaval for Edith and the girls – now three of them, since the arrival of Debby

---

1. Ibid, p. 246.

in 1945. Fran had been granted a leave of absence from the church, but it meant that a temporary pastor had to be employed, and he and his wife would live in the Parsonage while Fran was away. So Edith and her sister Janet found accommodation for their two families on Cape Cod and they spent the summer months together there. Their other sister, Elsa, was also able to join them for a fortnight with her daughters, which meant a lovely, extended get-together of cousins, making memories at the beach. There were plenty of squabbles, but much fun was had! Looking back later, that time would seem even more precious, as it would not be long before the families were scattered further afield than ever.

Edith and the three girls missed Fran terribly, and looked forward to receiving his letters from all over Europe. Despite the busyness of his schedule, Fran was making time to drink in the history of the places he visited wherever possible, particularly relishing the opportunities to find out more about the rich Christian history of Europe. While in Geneva, he wrote: "As I was up in the old city I saw the site where Calvin had died. I also saw the great cathedral, St. Peter's, the church where Knox had preached, old Calvin College, and the Reformation monument – I found it all so thrilling! We have a great heritage, and I am glad for whatever part I have in carrying it on."

His appreciation of art also grew as he visited art galleries and museums in places like Paris, Venice and Amsterdam, thrilled to see the originals of masterpieces he had previously admired only in books. But there was little time for this sightseeing, as it was always squeezed in between numerous interviews, conferences and speaking engagements. Some of these were encouraging, but others depressed him terribly. In Oslo, Norway, Fran attended a conference of the World Council of Churches that left him very discouraged. It seemed that the leaders there were in favor of uniting churches in an "inclusive" way that did not guard against false, liberal teaching. Fran believed they were moving away from the teaching of the Bible, with the message that "anything Christian is good". He was thankful to find the local Baptist church on the Sunday morning, and wrote to Edith:

"It was good for my soul. I could have wept. I understood them better in Norwegian than the World Council people at the conference in English! … I came out feeling that I knew better what a meeting of saints in heaven is going to be like."

Another painful aspect of the trip was seeing the effects of the war as he travelled from country to country, witnessing many areas in ruins from bombing and people worn down from food rationing. The practicalities of traveling in this post war period were far from straightforward, and the overcrowding on trains and platforms was terrible.

The trip was tiring and often overwhelming, but there were also many high points. Although Fran's fears about advancing liberalism in the church were often confirmed, he also experienced the joy of meeting true brothers and sisters in Christ, men and women of many different nationalities. Despite the oceans between them, and the barriers of language and culture, the unity he felt with these fellow believers amazed him. It was an inspiring and transformative time in Fran's life. In one of his last letters home, he wrote: "The trip is ended. This has been the great spiritual experience of my life, second only to my conversion."[2]

The final drama of these three months away was to happen on Fran's flight back from Paris to New York. Fran had flown a lot by this stage, and could feel that something was going wrong with the engines halfway through the journey. The plane fell about 3,000 feet in just a few minutes, and a white-faced co-pilot urged the passengers to put on their life jackets. Fran was sitting next to a woman with two young children, and spent time comforting her and promising to help take care of the children. Unbeknown to him, a news announcement had already gone out in the U.S. that a plane was going down over the Atlantic. Edith had gathered the children, and they were fervently praying for Daddy's safety, just as he was praying on the plane. Remarkably, the failed engines eventually started again, and the plane made it safely to land. Afterwards, Fran asked the pilot about what had happened.

---

2. All quotations from Fran's letters are from *The Tapestry*, p. 252-271.

"Well," he replied, shaking his head. "It's a strange thing, something we can't explain. Only rarely do two motors stop on one wing, but you can make it a rule that when they do, they don't start again. We don't understand it."

"I can explain it," Fran said, boldly. "My Father in Heaven started it because I was praying."[3]

The man simply looked at him, with a strange expression on his face, and turned away.

When those three months were over, the whole family were relieved to be back together in their beloved St. Louis home and looked forward to a return to normality. However, it was a long time before Fran would feel anything close to "normal" again. The trip had exhausted him, mentally and physically. The gruelling schedule of meetings and long hours of writing up his findings, the constant traveling in difficult circumstances, and the irregular sleep and diet resulted in a complete breakdown. He had desperately missed the support and care of Edith, and now it was this that he depended upon through his gradual return to health. She fed him and nursed him, and protected him as much as possible from the demands of ministry and even family life until he was well again.

---

3. Colin Duriez, *Francis Schaeffer: An Authentic Life* (Crossway, 2008), p. 270.

A Nomadic Life

Eventually, when Fran's health was sufficiently recovered, he began to accept requests to come and speak of his findings in Europe. He visited different churches and Christian organizations, showing many of the slides he had taken and reporting back on his impressions of all that he had seen and heard over those three months. However, the family regarded the trip as an interesting, out-of-the-ordinary interlude, rather than a taste of things to come. They threw themselves back into life in St. Louis, welcoming the return to their church family there, and to the spacious parsonage they called "home". Edith was particularly enjoying the new ladies' Bible class that she had started, which had grown from being a literary group meeting in the library to a fully fledged Bible study. The women were spiritually hungry, and eagerly responded to the Bible teaching she gave them. The Schaeffers were soon caught up once more in the weekly whirl of meetings, sermon preparation, pastoral calls, children's work and much more. Priscilla and Susan were both happily settled in school.

However, it began to seem as though God might have other ideas about their future. Gradually, letters began to arrive from all over Europe, from people Fran had spoken with and others who had heard of his visit and sought contact with him. Edith would later say that "the gist of them seemed to be, 'Come over and help us.'" It was a hard plea to ignore. Many more churches in America were inviting Fran to come and speak about what he had seen and experienced on his trip. Finally, a direct request came from the Independent Board who had sent Fran to Europe in the first place: "We feel strongly that we should send someone to Europe to strengthen the things that remain, and the consensus is that the only ones we would send would be you and Edith."[1]

After much talking and praying, Fran and Edith decided they should go. But it was not an easy decision. They had envisaged remaining in St. Louis for the rest of their working lives. They had worked hard on building relationships and laying down roots. They had good friends, and so did the children … friends they had looked forward to journeying through life with. They had enjoyed their lovely house, with its striking stairway sweeping into the hall – where Edith had even pictured her daughters leaning over the rail as they threw their wedding bouquets down to a crowd of guests beneath! The last Christmas they spent there felt "painfully beautiful" to Edith, with the house full of dark red roses,

1. Ibid, p. 272.

the tree shining with lights and a fire blazing in the brick fireplace. Not having anticipated this abrupt change of plan, Priscilla's Christmas gift was a newly redecorated bedroom, with new wallpaper, paint and curtains, and a new bedspread Edith had made! And the girls had all received a very special antique doll's house, far too large to be taken with them. Stepping out into the unknown, from all that was familiar and known and loved … it was a hard thing to do. At the end of their last Sunday service, Edith escaped to the cellar and wept, too overcome with emotion to face all the goodbyes. She also grieved for Fran, whose sermon had been so stirring that day, worrying that his gift for preaching might be wasted in the new role that lay ahead of him.

First came a six-month period living back in Philadelphia with Fran's mother, during which Fran travelled and spoke about the work in Europe, the girls went to school and Edith took a correspondence course to prepare her to act as Fran's secretary when they went abroad. This strange transitional time was made harder by Bessie Schaeffer's intense disapproval of their plans and her tight-lipped perfectionism in the home. Then, when at last the time drew near for the family to set sail for Holland, Priscilla had to be admitted to the hospital with a mystery illness that had been developing for months! No cause could be found for the vomiting and stomach pains that had laid her low – until eventually a tall, handsome doctor passing by her bed showed an interest in her case and pronounced it to be "mesenteric adenitis". He told them she must have her appendix removed the following day. When Edith explained about their situation and their forthcoming departure, Dr. C. Everett Koop was even more attentive, and told them that he had just become a Christian himself! He was particularly struck by the telegram Fran sent his daughter just before her operation: "Dear Priscilla, Remember underneath are the everlasting arms. Love, Daddy."[2] He saw that the Schaeffers lived by the faith they professed, and that God was "real" to them.

Priscilla recovered quickly after surgery and they were able to leave as planned the following week, beginning what Edith called their "nomadic life". They set sail aboard the New Amsterdam, waved off by a large gathering of friends and family who would continue to be their prayer support through the years ahead. Edith had made the three girls matching outfits of navy and white, with matching turquoise bags full of toys, crayons and activities – which made them much easier to spot on board! Once they reached Rotterdam harbor, the family travelled to Scheveningen, a seaside resort where they were to stay for a few months before moving on to Switzerland more permanently. They shared two rooms in a cheap "pension"[3] where the food was poor and the portions tiny due to strict rationing. It was rather a "rude awakening" for those in the family who were new to Europe – as was the war

---

2. Ibid, p. 282.

3. "Pension" is a term for a guest house or boarding house, often used in continental European countries.

damage to buildings and the black teeth of many of the local children.

Fran spent most of this time commuting to Amsterdam, where he was involved in organizing a conference in August 1948 for the formation of the International Council of Christian Churches. It was during this conference that he made a friend for life, Hans Rookmaaker. Hans was looking for an American who could answer some of his questions about jazz music, saw Dr. Schaeffer and asked, "May I speak to you?" Fran agreed pleasantly; he had half an hour before his next meeting at 7:00 pm. As it turned out, they talked all night, Fran finally leaving his new friend's room at 4:00 am the next morning! The conversation had revolved around philosophy, history and most of all art, about which Hans was very knowledgeable. He would later become an art critic for two national newspapers, as well as a professor of art history. Fran and Hans found they had a great deal in common, even in the way that each had come to faith largely through their independent reading of the Bible. A deep and satisfying friendship was born.

Speaking with Hans deepened Fran's belief that you could learn a lot about a society and its way of thinking by understanding the art it produced. He believed that the arts could give Christians a lot of useful insight into the mindset of the time, which would better equip them to reach out to unbelievers. This set Fran apart from a lot of pastors and others from his theological background, who were suspicious or just indifferent about modern art and culture.

Once the conference in Amsterdam was over, the Schaeffers enjoyed a short vacation seeing Brussels and Paris before traveling to Lausanne in Switzerland, where they hoped to settle for a longer period. There was much excitement as the train carried them through the beautiful French countryside towards the Alps, and through the mountains into Switzerland. They all rushed from one side of the train to the other to find the better view, exclaiming at the stunning beauty of the landscape. It was a promising beginning to this new phase of their adventure.

However, when the family arrived at the pension that had been found for them in La Rosiaz, near Lausanne, their hearts sank. Once more, their family of five were to be squeezed into two rooms. Where would the children play? Where would they do office work? It was hard not to think of their spacious home in St. Louis, with its thirteen rooms … but no, that would not do. With a deep breath and a bit of imagination, they made the space work. One room became the children's, with a little box under the washbasin which served both as toy storage and a step for Debby to stand on when she brushed her teeth. Boxes under beds provided more storage. The other room served as Fran and Edith's bedroom by night, and office or living room by day – not to mention "church" on Sundays!

Edith wrote to her family, describing their new home:

The price is cheaper than other pensions, and the house is scrupulously clean. Madame Turrian is very kind and pleasant and the view is a gift of the Lord. The trolley line ends two houses away, so transportation is close. We are in the highest part of Lausanne, just outside of the city limits. We have country sounds and smells all around us, the smell of hay and pine trees, and the constant music of tinkling cowbells. Priscilla, Susan and Debby have very little indoor space, but the front garden goes downhill to a wall and has some lovely spots under the trees to play. The backyard goes straight up, and has a rabbit and chicken house in it. Priscilla is allowed to gather the two or three eggs that appear each day. The Lord is filling our needs in one way if not another![4]

Life at Madame Turrian's certainly had its challenges. For one thing, all the other occupants of the pension were in their eighties and nineties, and could not cope with much childish noise or behavior. The sound of children quarrelling, or even laughing, would usually provoke a loud "ssshhh!" being hissed along the corridor by an elderly neighbor. Nonetheless, the curly-haired, three-year old Debby soon managed to charm the older ladies and join their knitting circle, being given her own long lengths of wool to play with. When she wasn't there, she could often be found trailing around the kitchen after Madame Turrian, learning cooking and a lot of French along the way!

Meanwhile, the two older girls were sent to a local Swiss school where they were forced to muddle along as well as they could in French. Poor Susan came home one

---

4. Ibid, p. 288.

afternoon in despair: "Oh Mommy! I can't understand the children, and I can't understand the teacher, and now I can't even understand myself!"

On Sundays the furniture in Fran and Edith's bedroom was pushed back to make room for three chairs and a stool to be placed between the beds and the washbasin: it was time for church. In the morning, Fran would preach from a Bible text (having prepared as carefully as though preaching for a large congregation), they would sing hymns and have prayers. The evening was given to a "young people's service" that the children took turns in leading. In due course, they even welcomed a few others to these tiny services, including an American lady with two children and an English nanny living in Lausanne.

In terms of work, the task Fran had been given to do by his mission board was to "strengthen what remains". In practice, this meant a number of things, including a certain amount of making it up as they went along! Fran used some of the many contacts he had made during his tour of Europe, and a lot of time was spent writing and dictating letters (which Edith, as secretary, would type), as well as both studying French. Twelve year old Priscilla quickly learned to help with the filing. There were also trips and speaking engagements away, which typically involved a similar format. Fran would give an overview of church history, before describing the challenges the church now faced in their day, particularly the pressure to deny the absolute truth of the Bible. He would then talk about the need to teach biblical truth to children, and the importance of finding ways to do this outside of the church when necessary. (Fran was aware that there was often no local church where children were being faithfully taught from the Bible.) He and Edith would then model one of their "Children for Christ" classes, and encourage people to consider starting a similar class in their own homes.

Many people took up this challenge. In time, in response to an increasing demand, Fran and Edith produced a lot of teaching material to help those who were beginning to host "Children for Christ" classes, and this material was eventually translated into thirteen languages and used all over Europe. There were points when Fran and Edith wondered if this was to be God's primary work for them.

Despite the encouragements, these early months in Switzerland were strange and unsettling ones for the family. They had left a home they loved and a ministry that was obviously fruitful ... for what? In all honesty, none of them were completely sure. Even if Fran and Edith tried not to voice this uncertainty, a few months into their new life, Priscilla did.

"What are we doing here?" she asked, miserably. "Why did we come?"

Move to the Mountains

"Oh, Mommy! Daddy! Look – just look!"

The three girls raced up the steep path towards the chalet, exclaiming with delight at the pretty balconies and window boxes full of bright geraniums. It was to be their home for the whole summer! Their French teacher in Lausanne had impressed upon Edith the importance of a change in altitude during the summer months, particularly for the sake of the children's health. "All Swiss do it," she explained, with a shrug. The family didn't need much persuasion. After several weeks of illness at Madame Turrian's, the change was particularly welcome.

Once Edith had unlocked the door of the rented chalet, the children ran around exploring the place thoroughly, and every now and then a whoop of excitement could be heard as some new delight was discovered. The girls could barely contain their joy at having a whole house to themselves again! The biggest thrill, for Susan, was the thought of having her mother in the kitchen again. She had found the unfamiliar soups served at the pension to be a particular trial, and often had to eat her helpings cold, when stubbornness finally gave way to hunger.

The family had not long settled in before visitors began to arrive for afternoon tea and conversation, beginning with a group of English schoolgirls Priscilla met at the local swimming pool. They soon returned, bringing others, and Edith had the opportunity to show their teacher some of the "Children for Christ" material she had written.

The summer passed pleasantly, but too swiftly. However, a short time before the family were due to return to Lausanne, they received an invitation to a place called Chalet Bijou, to meet with a German baroness who was staying there. Unsure of what to expect, they called upon her, and soon found that Baroness von Dumreicher was far from the formidable personage she might have sounded. She was a frail old lady, hard of hearing, who had fallen into hard times after a life of wealth and pleasure. She told Fran and Edith of her decadent lifestyle in Egypt, where she had lived for forty years. Yet recent years had brought much sorrow, as she had tragically lost several of her family members, including, finally, her husband and all her earthly possessions.

Here she leaned forward earnestly, her eyes bright with unshed tears.

"When I look back, I know that I've lived an empty life," she explained, sadly. "I know death cannot be far away. And I am afraid. I am afraid because I feel that there is so little time left to make up for it … "

Fran nodded his understanding, but smiled, as he leaned forward and gently took her fragile hand in his.

"But, Baronness," he assured her. "The Bible tells us that forgiveness for our sins is available – and that it does not depend upon anything we can do … no matter how much time we have. It depends only on what has already been done for us … by the Son of God, when He gave His life for us upon the cross."

The Baronness had to hold her earphone out to catch all of his words, and she continued to do so eagerly as Fran and Edith explained to her the good news of the gospel. Soon afterwards, she became a Christian, and was as delighted as a child, overflowing with the joy of freedom from guilt and fear. Edith thought once more of the pilgrim's burden of "sin" that had fallen down the stairs in her childhood game, and the feeling of lightness that followed. Now that joy belonged to the Baronness, for her burden was gone.

"Why do we have to go back?" moaned the children, as the end of the summer drew near. Fran and Edith thought about this, and realized that there was no reason really … at least, none that was insurmountable. Here they could rent a whole house for the same price as two rooms at Madame Turrian's. So much of Fran and Edith's work at the time involved traveling anyway; they could simply change their base to the village of

Champéry. That is … if God could provide them with a school for the girls, and a different chalet, since the one they were staying in had already been rented for the winter! And sure enough, God answered both prayers, although they had to wait until their final day in Champéry. Having found a school, but no chalet to live in, Edith was on the verge of giving up when she ran into the sister of their French teacher on the village street, who promptly offered them a chalet they could rent for a whole year. "Chalet des Frênes" was a beautiful, spacious house – fully furnished, with a lovely garden and all the character of an English country cottage. The family felt overwhelmed by this gift from God. It was the closest thing to a home they had known since leaving St. Louis, and finally they began to unpack the many boxes that had remained in storage since then. They were delighted to be reunited with things long forgotten, especially favorite books that seemed like old friends!

There were other clear signs that God had plans for the Schaeffer family in Champéry. Opportunities to share the gospel soon began to arise, sometimes in the most unexpected ways.

It was two days before Christmas and Edith and the girls were busy decorating the freshly cut tree when the doorbell rang. It was a young French pastor, calling to see the "American Protestant Pastor" he had been told about. It seemed that some Protestant Christians, visiting this Roman Catholic village for the holiday season, had asked if there might be a Christmas service they could go to in English.

Though more than willing to help, Fran immediately wondered where such a service could be held. He was told that there was an unused chapel in Champéry, built with money left by an English woman who had always spent her holidays there. If someone would provide wood for a fire, the chapel could be used – and the village hairdresser would play the organ!

The whole family were excited by this turn of events, not least little Debby, who stood on her head on the couch and exclaimed happily: "Daddy is going to preach in a really, truly church with lots of people there! I can't 'member a really, truly church with Daddy preaching!" And to their surprise, that icy cold Christmas morning, there really were a lot of people there. The service was a success, and permission was sought to hold more services. Fran soon found himself preaching there every Sunday morning, while Edith busily designed adverts to put up in all the various hotels and pensions to draw the attention of English-speaking tourists.

A regular group of school girls came along to these services, and when Fran spoke to them he discovered that they were at a Swiss "Finishing School" which always rented a large hotel in the mountains for the winter season, so that the pupils could both study and ski. Many of the girls seemed to be interested in talking more about Christianity, so with the permission of the school's Director, Fran and Edith soon invited them back to their home for regular evenings of tea, cake and conversation. The living room would often be full to bursting with young women from all over the globe – from India, Czechoslovakia, Canada, the U.K., South America and many other places. The discussions were so popular that Fran made the decision to postpone trips away until the spring. God was bringing people to them, right there in Champéry, and it seemed more important to stay.

"Is he here yet?" Debby demanded, impatiently, for what felt like the fiftieth time.

She was jumping from one foot to the other in anticipation, and Susan and Priscilla looked equally excited. Edith smiled at them, shaking her head.

"Not yet!" she laughed, glancing up at the kitchen clock. "But look, the train should be just pulling in. Why don't you all run and meet him on his way back up?

They were expecting a very special visitor, a young Norwegian named Christian. They had never met him, but their good friend the Baronness had told them more than enough to arouse their interest. She had moved back to Lausanne now, but they visited when they could, and on their last visit they had heard of nothing but Christian.

"He's a wonderful young man, a medical student," she had said, her eyes lighting up as she spoke of him. "So tall! He lives alone, you know, and looks after himself very well, washing his clothes and cooking and helping his landlady as part of the payment for his room. But even with that and all his studies, he still finds time to visit me, a sick old lady! He makes me tea, and plumps up my pillows and we talk … but mostly I talk, and he listens, for he speaks slowly, and only when he has thought carefully first."

The Schaeffers had eagerly issued an open invitation for Christian to visit and spend the weekend with them in the mountains.

When the girls returned, breathless, to the house, they brought with them a blonde-haired, blue-eyed boy of six foot six. He was beaming from ear to ear as his gaze took in the crisp white snow, the chalet and the welcoming family who lived there.

"Oh, it's just like home!" he declared, as Edith ushered them in from the cold.

Christian turned out to be the ideal house guest, helpful and charming. He did everything from shovelling snow, to washing up, to telling Norwegian fairy tales around the fireplace to an audience of enraptured girls. Despite his name, Christian was not a believer in the Lord Jesus, but he was happy to attend the church service on Sunday, and on Sunday evening he listened in on the usual discussions with the schoolgirls who came. Once they had left, the conversation continued, and thoughtful Christian began to ask some questions of his own.

Sadly, that wonderful weekend had to come to an end, but it was only the beginning of their friendship with Christian. More importantly, it was only the beginning of Christian's interest in finding out about the God of the Bible, and a few months later the Schaeffer family shared his joy as he came to know Jesus for himself.

For Fran and Edith, it was another confirmation that the Lord had brought them to Champéry for a reason. He had work for them to do there.

Fair Skies and Dark Clouds

Betty and Gea had heard a lot about the Schaeffers from Baronness von Dumreicher ... but somehow they hadn't taken in the fact that they were missionaries. If they had, they might have thought twice about this weekend visit. But now there was nothing to be done. It was getting dark as they crossed a wooden bridge across a rushing stream, and little Debby assured them that they were almost there.

"This is Chalet Bijou," she soon announced, proudly. "We used to live in Chalet les Frênes till it was sold. But now we love it here even more. It's where we very first met the Baronness, you know!"

Once their kindly young hostess had led them to a guest room and left them to get settled, the girls looked at one another in open dismay.

"Missionaries!" Betty moaned. "Oh dear! Some fun this turned out to be!"

At first the Schaeffers confirmed their worst fears. The long prayers, the constant talking about spiritual matters and the family's ignorance of the latest music and movies the girls mentioned … it was all a bit much! But gradually, Betty and Gea began to admire the warmth and sincerity of their hosts. They were struck by the family's closeness, and their enjoyment of simple pleasures. And gradually, they began to take an interest in the deep discussions that went on, often late into the night. The visit went on into the following week, and on Tuesday the two girls sat with Fran around the stove in the dining room for hours, their conversation turning into a full on Bible study in the book of Romans. Fran was in his element, for he had never forgotten how it felt to be the one asking the questions, or his amazement in discovering the Book that held all the answers.

Before the girls left, Betty followed Edith as she went off after breakfast to make the beds.

"I see it all now," she said, earnestly. "And I've come to believe that the Bible really is true. I want to accept Jesus now, Mrs. Schaeffer … please will you pray with me?

And although she didn't speak to them of it at the time, Gea's message in the guest book confirmed that she too had come to know Jesus.

By this time, through God's grace, the family had been given the opportunity to celebrate several such "new births". Through the regular school visits, and through word of mouth, a steady stream of visitors had made their way to the village of Champéry, first to

Chalet les Frênes and then to Chalet Bijou, to enjoy the Schaeffer's hospitality and to ask their questions about faith. But there would soon be a new birth of a different kind to celebrate, for Edith was expecting another baby. The girls were being particularly protective of their mother, since she had suffered a miscarriage not long before.

"We want this baby," they told her, firmly. "We're going to look after you, and you're going to put your feet up!"

Of course there was still plenty of work to be done, but Debby would almost push her mother down onto the couch if she showed any sign of weariness, thrusting pillows under her feet.

"You need to have your feet higher than your head! We don't want anything to happen to our baby."

Susan did her part by making a huge, illustrated poster entitled "What Expectant Mothers Should Eat" and hanging it in a prominent place in the dining room.

Thankfully, it wasn't long before the girls awoke to the news that their new baby brother had safely arrived, and at once tiptoed into the bedroom to greet the little bundle with delight and awe. Every day, once school hours were done, baby Franky had three extra "mothers" to help look after him.

"Mom-mmy!" whined Franky, fretfully, not sounding at all his usual, boisterous two-year old self. "Tummy hurts, kiss it! Tummy hurts, kiss it!"

The family were onboard ship, on their way back to Switzerland after an eighteen month furlough in America. It was the last night onboard when little Franky began to suffer excruciating stomach pains. He soon started vomiting, on and on until he finally fell asleep in Edith's arms. To their relief, he seemed a little better the following day; it wasn't until the morning after, during a brief stopover in Paris, that Edith saw to her horror her lively little boy was struggling to walk. He stumbled as he tried to make his way across the hotel room, and then collapsed completely.

"Can't walk, Mommy ... can't walk!" he cried.

It was decided that Edith and Franky must fly back to Switzerland straight away, instead of traveling by train with the rest of the family. Although he needed to see a doctor urgently, the Schaeffers felt it was best to try to get to one they knew and trusted. In the end, however, it was impossible to get in touch with their own doctor, and Edith was forced to take Franky to another man in Aigle, who made light of the situation.

"It's just a virus," he reassured Edith, but she found that hard to believe.

Soon the family were all reunited at Chalet Bijou – a subdued homecoming, despite their happiness to be back. The following day, another doctor came out to see Franky, a specialist, and immediately pronounced it to be polio, a serious viral infection that children are vaccinated against nowadays. At that time, however, it was common and could be life-threatening. The doctor ordered hour-long hot baths and massage, which were continued throughout that winter. Thankfully, Franky gradually recovered and was able to walk again, although he would face lifelong complications due to the loss of muscle in his lower left leg.

That winter was a testing time for the whole family. To make matters worse, in October, Susan fell ill with rheumatic fever and was confined to bed for a period of two months, which in reality would extend to three years, on and off. There was a lot of extra work for Edith and Priscilla in caring for the two invalids, but the ministry at Chalet Bijou resumed nonetheless. Regular afternoon teas and evening discussions were still held, as well as the Bible class Priscilla helped to teach in French for the local children.

Another dark cloud hung over those winter months, for Fran and Edith had not yet received their permit to continue living and working in Switzerland. This had to be renewed every six months, and there had never been a delay before. Certain rumors reached their ears, that there was a problem with their permits because of their "Protestant" ministry in a Roman Catholic area. But most of the villagers dismissed these rumors, and Fran and Edith did not know what to think as they waited anxiously for news. They couldn't believe that God would want them to think about moving; on the contrary, they felt excited about their work in Champéry and the way it was developing. As they looked back over their years there, they could see that

God was bringing to them an increasing number of people with spiritual hunger. The harvest was plentiful.

"Dear Lord," prayed Edith one day, as she sat at her typewriter, struggling to concentrate. "Please give me the comfort and peace I need today."

She reached for her Bible and began to read from the book of Isaiah, not by coincidence but because it was where she had got to in her daily readings. And there, in chapter 2 verse 2, she read these words: "And it shall come to pass in the last days, that the mountain of the Lord's house shall be established in the top of the mountains, and shall be exalted above the hills; and all nations shall flow unto it. And many people shall go and say, Come ye, and let us go up to the mountain of the Lord, to the house of the God of Jacob; and he will teach us of his ways, and we will walk in his paths."

Edith instantly felt a rush of excitement. She knew God was speaking to her through these words. The idea of a place in the mountains, where people could come from all over the world to seek God and truth. This was the place she and Fran had been thinking of … he had even come up with a name for it, "L'Abri", the French word for "shelter". Surely, that place was here at Chalet Bijou. Surely, God was confirming that this was the ministry that lay ahead of them; indeed, that had already begun! Joyfully, she got her pencil and wrote in the margin beside the verse God had given her: "Jan '55, promise … Yes, L'Abri".

* * *

"Monsieur and Madame Schaeffer, Priscilla, Susan and Deborah must leave Champéry, and the Canton of Valais by midnight the night of March 31 … "

Looking up at Fran in disbelief, Edith reached for the second sheet of paper he held out to her.

"Monsieur and Madame Schaeffer, Priscilla, Susan and Deborah must leave all of Switzerland by midnight the night of March 31, not to return for the space of two years … "

The same reason was given on both letters. Their crime was "having had a religious influence in the village of Champéry."

"But — it isn't possible!" Edith exclaimed, in disbelief. The shocked faces of the rest of the family mirrored her own. Her eyes met Fran's as they both shared the unspoken question: what about L'Abri?

Living by Faith

"As I see it," said Fran, slowly, his voice breaking into the stunned silence. "There are two courses of action open to us. We could hurry to send telegrams to Christian organizations, our Senator in Washington, and so on, trying to get all the human help we could possibly get; or we could simply get down on our knees, and ask God to help us. It seems to me that we are being given an opportunity right now to demonstrate God's power. Do we believe God is able to do something in government offices, in this present situation, as He was able in times past? Do we believe our God is the God of Daniel? If so, we have an opportunity to prove it now."[1]

Fran's resolve to live by prayer had strengthened during their years at Chalet Bijou. During their early months there, he had been through something of a "crisis of faith". This was partly because of wider conflicts within their church denomination in the U.S., which Fran inevitably got drawn into despite his geographical distance. He was unhappy with the

---

1. Edith Schaeffer, *L'Abri* (Tyndale House, 1969, p. 78.

contrast between the Christian principles at stake, and the decidedly unchristian attitudes with which people (including, at times, himself) disagreed and argued over them. Discouraged, he had even begun to re-examine the very foundations of his faith. He needed to take time by himself, to think, pray and read the Bible. When the weather was fine, he would go off hiking alone; when it was bad, he would pace up and down the hayloft at Chalet Bijou, wrestling with his doubts, going back to the very roots of his faith to answer again those same questions he had asked as a teenager: Who is God? Who are we? Why are we here?

It was an anxious time for Edith, who could only keep praying for her husband, not knowing what the outcome of this soul searching was going to be. Yet the Holy Spirit had worked powerfully in Fran's life through those weeks, and he emerged from it with a stronger faith than ever. He was even more convinced of the truths of Christian teaching, truths that were strong enough to stand under thorough investigation. Yet he also had a stronger personal relationship with God, and a deeper sense of the importance of living by faith day by day, relying completely upon Jesus. And here, in this present crisis, was an opportunity to do just that.

So the first thing the Schaeffers did was to get on their knees and pray, as a family, each one aloud in turn, right down to little Franky. "Dear Heavenly Father, please show us what to do." "Oh God, let us stay if it be thy will." "Dear Lord, guide us."

* * *

By the end of a long day of house hunting, Edith was in near despair. They had only ten days to appeal against their eviction from Switzerland, and had been told that they could only do so if they could give an address, in a Protestant canton which was prepared to let them stay. This had led them to the mountain village of Villars, in Vaud. But everything in Villars was way out of their price range, and time was running out. Exhausted and tearful, Edith began to pray.

"Oh Lord, if you want us to stay in Switzerland, if your word to me concerning L'Abri means our being in these mountains, then I know you are able to find a house, and lead me to it in the next half hour. Nothing is impossible to you."[2]

As she continued wearily down the main street of Villars, Edith suddenly heard her name called.

"Madame Schaeffer, avez-vous trouve quelque chose?" (Have you found anything?)

It was a real estate dealer whom they had spoken to several days before, who had been unable to help them.

"Non, Monsieur."

He gestured to his car and opened the door. "Come on, I think I have something that might interest you."

He drove Edith out of Villars and down the mountainside to a small village called Huémoz a few minutes away. Heavy fog hid the view so that Edith could get little sense of the location, but as

---

2. Ibid, p. 92.

she looked around the fully furnished, three-floored chalet her hopes began to rise a little. That was, until she remembered to ask: "Monsieur, how much is the rent, please?"

"Oh, it's not for rent," he answered. "It's for sale."

For sale! The momentary hope she had allowed herself seemed to be dashed. Here was a suitable place – and within half an hour, as she had prayed. Yet they didn't have anything like the kind of money to buy it. And besides, it would be madness to buy a house in a country they still didn't have a permit to live in ... wouldn't it?

Over the next few days, Fran and Edith became increasingly sure that was exactly what God wanted them to do. Sums of money, large and small, began to come in from unexpected sources. The Schaeffers had not asked for money, although many prayer supporters in America and elsewhere knew of their work. Some of their benefactors wrote of the strong urges they had felt to send the money, often in very particular amounts, and to do so right now. The girls made a chart in the form of a thermometer to record the total and updated it each time a new gift arrived, so that the whole family were waiting in eager expectation to see what God would do. For Fran and Edith, it was a wonderful confirmation of God's guidance, leading them in a direction they had never intended, but could not doubt was His will.

So, miraculously, when the family moved out of Champéry, as ordered, on March 31st, 1955, it was to Chalet les Mélèzes in Huémoz that they went. It was late in the evening when they arrived, Susan and a family friend having gone ahead the day before to make up beds and organise some food. So it wasn't until the following morning that the family woke up to the glorious view God had given them ... the view that had been hidden by fog on the day of Edith's visit!

They wasted no time moving a small table and breakfast things out on to one of the balconies so that they could enjoy it while they ate. It was truly breathtaking. The chalet looked right down across the Rhône Valley, with the river winding down below. They counted fourteen villages and towns hugging the mountainside on either side. Beyond the valley rose snow-topped peaks, and behind the chalet, steep grassy meadows that led into deep pine woods. At the front of their own lawn was a twenty-foot drop to the road where the bus stopped – right outside their house. This was the bus that connected with the train to Aigle, and from there one could travel almost anywhere – Lausanne, Geneva, London, Paris, Milan. Having previously had a mile-long, difficult walk to the station from Chalet Bijou, this felt like another marvellous gift.

"That will make it much easier to travel from here," Fran observed, pleased. They were thinking mostly of their own trips, the speaking engagements and conferences, and of Priscilla who hoped to enrol in the University at Lausanne. They had little idea, then, just how significant those transport links would be for many other people as well.

On June 21st, it was officially confirmed: the Schaeffers were allowed to stay in Huémoz. Their passports were returned, and they could finally breathe a sigh of relief and begin to think about the future of their work at Chalet les Mélèzes: "L'Abri". Fran had now resigned from his Mission Board, so the family were really stepping out on their own, in faith. But without the young people coming from Champéry schools for tea and discussions, without the church services ... what exactly would their work be?

They weren't left to wonder for long, for visitors soon began to come. First, it was an American friend whom Priscilla brought home from University; Grace, a glamorous but discontented girl with many questions about the Christian faith. The same weekend two other young girls joined them, the daughter of American friends and another student she was hitchhiking with. On the Friday evening after dinner, conversation continued by candlelight and went on until two in the morning. After lunch the following day, another long conversation, then a hike and toasting hot dogs round an outdoor fire in the evening.

It was a pattern that continued. Priscilla brought more and more friends back for weekends, often students who had approached her to talk about Christianity. Two young artists came to stay for a week, spending time sketching local scenes as well as discussing faith with Fran, Edith and even Susan. As it happened, Phyllis, one of the young artists, was the first to come to faith at "L'Abri", after several intense conversations with Fran.

"I'm not sure what Christianity meant to me before, but I know what it means to me now," she said, fervently, after she had prayed with them to accept Jesus as her Savior and Lord. As she boarded the bus, her face was radiant.

L'Abri

"Why don't you come up to Huémoz with me this weekend?" Grace asked John, casually. "There's a nice American family there, sort of a house party. You'd like it."

John agreed to come. He was Swiss by birth, but had grown up in New York so he felt very at home amongst Americans. Besides, it would be good to have a break from studying. But as he waited at the train station on Friday afternoon, he was somewhat taken aback when Grace rushed up to him at the last minute to explain, breathlessly, "I'm coming up later with Dick on his motorbike. You go on though!"

So John travelled to Aigle alone. At the station, he overheard a young American, also trying to buy a ticket to Huémoz. Clearly this man spoke little French and was struggling to make himself understood. John stepped forward to help, to the American's evident relief. When he realized that the man had no Swiss francs either, John bought tickets for them both.

"It seems we're heading to the same place," said John, grinning. "I'm John Sandri."

"Karl Woodson," answered the American, warmly, shaking his hand. "Thanks a lot for that. I've come over from an army base in Germany. I'm on my way to visit some folks I used to know back in St. Louis."

The two young men chatted easily on the bus, soon realizing they were headed not only to the same village, but to the very same chalet. Unlike Karl, John still had no real idea who the Schaeffers were, or what they were doing in Huémoz. When they arrived at Chalet les Mélèzes, Fran was waiting to meet them at the gate, keen to make the most of the last daylight hours before dinner. Once introductions had been made, he suggested they go for a walk, and talk.

As they started out, the first part of the conversation between Fran and Karl passed John by; he was too busy drinking in the clean mountain air and admiring the spectacular view. But he soon caught on to a mention of Christianity.

"Oh, but I don't think Christianity has a leg to stand on intellectually, do you, Mr. Schaeffer?" John interjected, innocently enough.

The answer he received lasted two hours! In fact, John did a lot of listening that weekend. On the Sunday evening before he left, he wrote in the guest book: "My eyes have been opened to a new world in which I hope to dwell with a coming faith!" Being a thorough sort of person, John didn't jump into a commitment but took away the set of Bible studies Fran had written and worked through them over the summer. It was

November before he returned to L'Abri, with the happy news that he had indeed put his faith in Jesus! Two and a half years later, after they had both graduated from the University of Lausanne, he would marry Priscilla Schaeffer in the first L'Abri wedding. A few years after that, having undertaken further theological studies, the couple would return to live and work at L'Abri themselves for many years.

John and Grace were just two of the many students from the university who visited L'Abri, weekend by weekend. The interest was such that by November, Fran was also going to Lausanne to run a weekly Bible and discussion class for students at a local café. But there were others too. In the earliest weeks of L'Abri, two young nurses from Virginia named Anne and Mary had visited, and they went on to bring many medical people from Basel where they were studying, students of many different nationalities and backgrounds. They would often bring a car full; and due to lack of space, that first year it was common for several mattresses to be spread out on the living room floor and quickly rolled up to rearrange the room for "church" on the Sunday morning.

Once Fran had formally resigned from his Mission Board, he and Edith had spent time praying over L'Abri and agreeing some key principles about how it would be run. The four main principles were these:

They would pray for God to meet their financial and material needs, without sending out pleas for money;

They would pray for God to send the people of His choice to them, and keep others away;

They would pray that God would plan the work, and unfold His plan to them day by day, rather than trying to plan the future themselves;

They would pray that God would send them the workers of His choice to help with the work, rather than advertising in the usual way.

It wasn't that the Schaeffers felt this was the only way mission work should be approached, but they believed it was the right course for them and for L'Abri. They wanted to make sure that what went on there was truly God's work, rather than their own. They also wanted the unbelievers who visited to be influenced not only by the discussions, but by seeing in practice what it looked like to trust God day by day, and to see Him answer prayer.

Fran and Edith called the work "The L'Abri Fellowship", and began to distribute regular "Family Letters" which Edith faithfully wrote for many years, and which would be sent out to a growing number of people as the years went on. Her father, George Seville, had just retired and gladly agreed to serve as a "Home Secretary", dealing with administration on the American side. Her mother Jessie undertook the work of copying and distributing Edith's letters to those who were supporting them in prayer. Their first official "worker" was Priscilla, who juggled this with her University studies, soon followed by a young American friend Dorothy Jamison, who ended up staying and living with the family for two years before marrying another early L'Abri worker, Hurvey Woodson – the brother of Karl.

Even with this help and support, it was obvious from the beginning that the work at L'Abri was not going to be easy. God was faithful in meeting their needs, but this certainly did not mean living in luxury, particularly during the early years. There was no regular source of income to rely on, and Fran and Edith were determined not to ask those who visited to pay for anything; they wanted them to feel like family. But often they had very little, and had to make it go a long way. It wasn't unusual for them to eat porridge for two of their daily meals. Heating was also a problem, and it was always very cold. Hurvey was told to sit near to the fireplace during the long discussions, guarding the wood block to make sure visitors didn't add too much wood to the fire! Fran would often go through the ashes in the fireplace, fishing out any pieces of coal that could be used again.

It was also challenging for the family to share their home and lives so completely with other people. For one thing, it meant a lot of hard work, most of it decidedly unglamorous: endless stacks of dishes to wash, meals to prepare, sheets to hang out, toilets to clean. As word about L'Abri spread, this "place in the mountains where one could get answers", unexpected guests frequently arrived at unexpected times! They were always welcomed, but it meant that any sort of ordinary family life was difficult, to say the least.

Edith and Debby walked through the door laden with shopping bags from their trip to the market in Villars, bringing the fog in with them. Priscilla was waiting excitedly in the kitchen.

"They're here!" she whispered, loudly. "And they're not some kind of gospel singers, they're opera singers!"

All the family had been told, by telegram, was that two singers were coming for Easter weekend, friends of a missionary they knew in Italy. They had no idea what to expect. Edith and Debby put down their bags and went quickly downstairs to meet their new guests.

"Thank you for having us at such short notice," said the glamorous, smiling lady who was warming herself by the fire. "Georgia has told us so much about you all."

Jane was a tall, impressive-looking soprano with a personality to match. Anita, her friend, was tiny, and spoke little, although that may have been because Jane did enough talking for both of them! That evening over dinner, she kept them all in stitches telling hilarious stories about her experiences in the world of opera. But she didn't just talk about herself. She wanted to know all about them, and Edith ended up telling the whole story of how they had been sent away from Champéry and how L'Abri had come into existence.

That weekend everyone grew to like Jane more and more. She was full of energy and enthusiasm, and despite her glamorous career was perfectly happy to muck in with everything. She washed dishes, read aloud to little Franky and entertained the girls with stories. She was delighted with the woods and the village, and listened eagerly to Fran speak about Jesus.

"But what about other religions?" she asked at one point, clearly troubled by this. "I've met so many sincere followers of other faiths ... surely God will accept them too?"

Fran gently explained to Jane that all the major religions teach very different things about God, and therefore they can't all be right.

"Jesus says, 'I am the way and the truth and the life. No man cometh to the Father but by me,'" Fran told her, showing her the verse in his Bible. "We might find that difficult to accept. But Jesus is the only one who can offer forgiveness of sins, and without that forgiveness we cannot have a restored relationship with God. In all other religions, we have to work to earn our salvation. The Bible says that is impossible. We could never do enough. Instead, it offers us a Savior, who alone can do it for us."

Jane stayed a day longer than she had intended, and when she left everyone was sorry to see her go. But they received a long letter from Milan a few days later with thrilling news.

"When Georgia spoke of you and mentioned a possibility of a visit, I was the least interested, and later said quite flatly that I'd never find the time for such a thing. Now I am perfectly certain that I was led to L'Abri by a power quite outside myself, which now I am able to believe was the Holy Spirit, leading me forward in God's plan for my life. Indeed, I feel that the power of Christ's Spirit has opened my blinded eyes to the true light."[1]

Jane became a frequent visitor to L'Abri. She brought many friends with her, but had many others who weren't able to travel to Huémoz, so she and Anita soon asked Fran if he might be able to run another discussion group, in Milan. He agreed, and so added this fortnightly trip to his already busy timetable! It was worth it for the opportunity to share the gospel with another huge range of people with different backgrounds, and of different nationalities. Many of them were involved in music or the theater professionally and were very unlikely to have had much connection with the church, but were open to hearing what Fran had to say in a neutral, non-religious setting. Over time, people came to put their faith in Jesus and the small group of believers there grew.

As for Jane, her faith went from strength to strength. She continued to talk to others about Jesus and invite them along to the discussion group. She read her Bible avidly, and many other Christian books and biographies which stirred her heart. But as she did so, a conflict began to grow inside her. She had spent her whole life preparing for a career in opera, and now she had

1. Ibid, p. 150.

"made it"; she was a success. Should she go on in that profession, using her talent now to God's glory? At first that seemed like the right path, but as time went on Jane felt increasingly uncomfortable with her glamorous career.

One day, as she was reading her young niece a Bible story, she noticed the girl was looking up at her with shining eyes.

"Oh, Aunt Jane, when you are old and your voice is cracked – you know what you ought to be, you ought to be a missionary!"

Those words stayed with Jane, but in the end she couldn't wait – and she knew God didn't want her to wait. He wanted her to demonstrate her trust in Him by giving it all up now … even while her voice was at its best. So she went to be a worker at L'Abri, and later she sold all her wonderful opera costumes so that the money could be used to help fund the building of a chapel there.

The Work Grows

It was not unusual for the family to receive gifts that were designated for particular purposes, and when they did so it was always a great encouragement to their faith. They had determined early on that the work at L'Abri should proceed according to God's plan, not their own, and these gifts seemed to confirm that He was indeed directing their course.

When they had first arrived at Chalet les Mélèzes, it had lacked a living room suitable for the long, relaxed discussions that were so central to their ministry. Two doctors from the U.S. turned out to be God's agents in meeting this need. One, a tuberculosis specialist, felt God leading him to send a certain amount of money to L'Abri, which corresponded exactly with the quote for the building work to create that living room. The second, the head of a children's hospital, had followed the story of L'Abri with great interest through the "Family Letters", and wrote that he would like to give a sum of money that would allow a fireplace to be built in that living room.

Answers to prayer were not always "yes". When faced with the ongoing need for more space, one thing they considered was trying to buy a chalet on the back road that became available. Yet in that case, the deadline date passed without the Schaeffers receiving the money necessary to buy it, and so it was sold to someone else. Instead, they embarked on the building of a new room where a patio had previously been. Here was another test of faith. There was money enough to begin the job, but not to complete it.

"Monsieur Schaeffer," said the mason, one chilly October afternoon. "We need to know if you want us to finish this job. If I order all the stone at the same time, I can get it at a reduced rate for you."

Fran shrugged. "I'm sorry, Monsieur," he answered, sincerely. "At the moment, we have enough for the foundation and the walls, but not the rest of the job. We never borrow money; we trust God to provide it when the time is right."

Monsieur Bratschi shook his head in bemusement at this crazy American.

"But, Monsieur Schaeffer," he persisted. "If this freezing weather continues, we will soon be putting off all the outside work until the spring. And in a few days, we have another job we simply must go to."

"We'll pray about it and let you know as soon as we can," Fran promised.

They held a "Day of Prayer" the very next day. At the top of the chart of names and times, Susan had written out this verse from Jeremiah 32:17: "Ah Lord God! Behold, thou hast made the heaven and the earth by thy great power and stretched out arm, and there is nothing too hard for thee."

When the mail arrived, Fran summoned everyone to the dining room – the family, the current L'Abri workers and even the few guests who were currently with them. He handed Edith a letter to read aloud, from a lady who had visited L'Abri herself and was very aware of the need for more space. She enclosed a sum that she wished to be used for that particular purpose. A sum that enabled Fran to go outside and tell the workmen to go ahead, order the stone and finish the job! That Day of Prayer ended with a time of heartfelt thanksgiving.

L'Abri was growing. The chalet itself was growing, and more visitors than ever were making the journey up to Huémoz to ask their questions. But Fran Schaeffer's influence was also beginning to extend further afield. There were now regular discussion groups being held in Basel, Lausanne, Milan and even Holland. As they had agreed, there was never any advertising, but through word of mouth the message was spreading. It was not that it was a new message: on the contrary, what Fran taught was the gospel of Jesus Christ crucified, the same gospel the apostles had proclaimed in New Testament times. But Fran's unique gift was in getting to the heart of people's objections against the Christian faith. He really listened to their questions, and took the time to answer them thoughtfully. In his personal study time, he read widely, continuing to pursue his interests in philosophy, art and modern culture, as well as theology. Unlike many other "religious" figures at the time, he sought to understand how young people thought, and to get alongside them. Because of that, they respected him, and they listened to him.

"I have appendicitis," Franky announced importantly, to the visitor at his bedside. Then he paused for a moment, his small features forming a perplexed frown. "No, that's not right … hepatitis. No, I mean bronchitis! I'm always getting mixed up around here. We have so many things, I can't remember which one I have!"

March of 1958 was a difficult month at L'Abri. Several family members and L'Abri workers were laid low with various illnesses, and in one case a broken leg – which meant there was a lot of nursing to do and less hands on deck to help with all the practical work. Yet there was still a steady flow of visitors arriving, who were never turned away. Added to this was mounting concern over the finances. With extra medical bills to be paid and no monetary gifts coming in the post, it was an anxious time.

The family were all glad of the arrival of their good friend Jane, who promptly suggested scheduling an extra morning of prayer. "Days of Prayer" had always been a regular part of L'Abri life – a list would go up

and people would put their names down for particular
time slots throughout the day so that at least one person
would always be praying. "I'll take two hours," Jane
declared, and the other slots soon filled up.

God did answer their prayers over the financial
needs of L'Abri, and wonderfully, by the time March's
bills came in, there was money enough to pay them.
However, one of the first letters that arrived following
that prayer morning wasn't quite what they had
expected. It told of a gift of money that had been
given by a young medic who had recently become a
Christian at L'Abri. But this money was not for use at
Chalet les Mélèzes; it had been set aside for a specific
purpose. Hilary had felt a particular urge to give a sum
of money that would enable the Schaeffers to make a
trip to England, and to spend some time speaking to
people there about Christianity in the same "informal"
way they did at L'Abri.

The England trip was soon planned for June of that
year. A hotel suite had been booked for Fran and Edith
near Marble Arch, in central London; a suite big enough
for them to receive and talk to people. Several English
friends who had been to L'Abri knew about the visit,
and had made it known to their friends and family, but
apart from that no particular plans had been made. The
only preparation for the visit was prayer; prayer that
God would send the people of His choosing to those
hotel rooms. And over the course of that week, over
seventy-five different people made their way there to

talk to the Schaeffers and ask questions, some of them returning several times. It felt to Fran and Edith like a tiny version of L'Abri in the teeming heart of London – albeit lacking the cosy fireside and alpine views!

One afternoon, the Schaeffers were invited to Cambridge, and Fran had the opportunity to give a short talk over tea in the living room of a student at St. Catherine's college. Unbeknown to them at the time, the tall, red-haired young student hosting them that afternoon would later become not only a worker at L'Abri but their own Susan's husband! A thoughtful, philosophical young man, Ranald Macaulay had recently become a Christian but still had many unanswered questions. He found himself roped into hosting the Schaeffers by a South African friend who had visited L'Abri and claimed it had changed her life. After a few minutes of pleasant enough conversation, Edith nudged her husband to remind him that he had something to say to these young people. With every eye in the room fixed upon him, Fran held up his hand. There was complete silence.

"The supernatural," he began, "Is as close to me as my hand."

Mesmerized, Ranald and his friends listened as Fran argued powerfully for the existence of God, and in discussion afterwards really engaged with their questions and doubts. This would be the first of many interactions with Cambridge students, which led to many more visits to the city for Fran and Edith, but also to many groups of British students making the "pilgrimage" to L'Abri ... students not only from Cambridge, but soon afterwards from Oxford, St. Andrew's and other universities. All of them found something unique in Fran's way of explaining the Christian faith. Fran had never lost the excitement he had felt discovering answers for himself in the Bible – that "fire in his bones"– and his excitement was contagious.

Wendy was a student at Lausanne who had recently become a Christian at L'Abri. She had been desperate for Fran and Edith to visit her unbelieving parents at their home in Surrey during their time in England, and it was there that Edith met Linette.

Linette was a young ballet dancer; a slender, attractive girl with a strange sadness in her eyes. Edith had little chance to speak to her individually, but she couldn't help noticing how attentively Linette listened when she related to their hostess the story of L'Abri, with an expression of something like wistfulness on her face. When they returned to Lausanne, Edith asked Wendy about Linette, and the story she heard prompted her to sit down and write to the young woman immediately. An only child, Linette had recently lost both her father and then her mother, who had taken her own life rather than continue without him. No wonder then the sadness in her eyes! Nor that hunger for something to put her hope in.

Edith invited her to L'Abri. "After what Wendy has told me, I feel you need a bit of home life, peace, joy and quiet ... before you go on into the next things you need to do."

Linette came straight away. After their first family dinner together, Fran noticed their guest alone on the balcony, weeping as she leaned against the rail with her head in her hands.

"Edith," he whispered, urgently. "Go out to Linette. I think she needs you."

Edith stopped the work she was doing, exchanging glances with Susan as she went. No words were needed: she knew that Susan and the others would take care of the work to be done, all the while praying for Linette and the work God was doing in her heart.

"I'm afraid," Linette admitted, brushing away tears with the back of her hand as Edith gently put her arm around her shoulders. "And lonely ... I'm so tired of being alone!"

During the course of that evening, she allowed Edith to share with her the good news of the Savior who promises never to leave those who trust in Him, but to be with them always, "even to the very end of the age." They talked for hours. Linette confessed that she had always thought the Bible was just a series of disconnected stories with no obvious unity. As they talked Edith explained how, despite its many different human authors and genres, the Bible gives one clear message. It is the message of a God who has intervened in human history to save lost and broken people. A message that is far from old and irrelevant, but is everything we need, the only thing that gives us the truth and hope we need today.

Around midnight, the miracle happened. The eyes of faith were opened, and a brilliant smile transformed Linette's face.

"You know … I'm not afraid anymore," she said, with a sense of wonderment. "And I'll never be alone again."

Linette insisted that her flat in Chelsea should be used by Fran and Edith during all their subsequent visits, instead of a hotel suite. So for those days, she would move out, and 59 Sloane Gardens would become the "little L'Abri of London". Later on, when, like Jane, Linette decided to give up her stage career and come to L'Abri as a worker, she suggested that someone should live in the flat permanently as a representative of L'Abri. From then on it officially became a L'Abri center in London, occupied at first by Hilary and then a succession of other workers. Much later, it would be replaced by a larger house in Ealing; and eventually, a manor house in Hampshire was bought and restored by a team of volunteers led by Ranald and Susan Macaulay, who would be L'Abri's English representatives there for many years.

Into the Limelight

"Mrs. Schaeffer!"

Edith turned around from the sink where she stood washing dishes to see John Boice, a L'Abri worker at that time, beckoning her over from the doorway. She hastily rubbed her wet hands on her apron as she went over to him, her curiosity aroused by the excited gleam in his eye.

"Mrs. Schaeffer, could you do me a favor? There's the most wonderful discussion going on in there —" he gestured to the living room with a flick of his head "— those girls from Smith College are asking some really interesting questions and Dr. Schaeffer is giving brilliant answers. I really think this should be recorded! I'm going to go unpack that tape recorder right now and set it up in the hall. But I need you to be a 'distraction' — please could you take in some tea and things, and just make an awful clatter setting everything up, so that no one will notice me hiding the mic in a plant pot and setting up the extension lead?"

Edith hesitated for a moment. She knew how Fran felt about being recorded. The tape recorder had been sent by a L'Abri prayer supporter more than six months before, but Fran was adamant that they had no use for it; he would never speak into a microphone, it would ruin the flow of the discussions and besides, people should be able to ask their questions in private. However, that evening she let herself be swayed by John's enthusiasm and played her part, taking in a tray of tea and cookies and making as much commotion as she could, despite Fran's look of bewildered irritation as he tried to ignore her and continue his discussion!

Fran might have been furious when he found out he had been recorded, if it hadn't been for the obvious delight of the college girls who had been asking the questions. When they heard about the secret recording the following day, they eagerly requested copies for themselves and for other friends. Fran's objections dissolved when he realized how useful this new tool could be. As far as he was concerned, anything that enabled more people to hear God's truth had to be a good thing! So that was the beginning of the tape programme. Over the next few years a substantial library of recorded Bible studies, talks and discussions was built up, and these were used extensively by visitors to L'Abri, particularly those who came to study there for longer periods of time. As demand for this grew, the Schaeffers rented a neighboring chalet which became "Farel House", a place people could go to read and study in more depth under Fran's guidance. Among the first to use it would be their future son-in-laws, Ranald

Macaulay from Cambridge and Udo Middelmann, a young law student from Germany who had become a Christian at L'Abri and would go on to marry Debby.

However, the tapes were also passed around and listened to much further afield than L'Abri. As a result, Francis Schaeffer's reputation continued to grow. Another influential factor in his increasing fame was an article written by a journalist from *Time* magazine whose daughter was at high school with Debby. He visited L'Abri with a photographer in 1959 and despite the Schaeffers' reluctance, published an article about the extraordinary Christian ministry that was going on there. In the article he described his visit: "The twenty-odd guests this week include an Oxford don, an engineer from El Salvador, a ballet dancer and an opera singer. The one thing they have in common is that they are intellectuals. And the European intellectual is the single object of the Schaeffers' mission in the mountains."[1]

It is unlikely that Fran and Edith would have been entirely happy with that assessment of their work, for the hospitality and Bible teaching at L'Abri were open to all, regardless of social class or background. Fran had not come from an "intellectual" environment himself, and was just as comfortable talking with laborers or soldiers as he was with professors or performers. Nevertheless, because of the deep discussions of culture, philosophy and ideas that often took place

---

1. Duriez, *Francis Schaeffer: An Authentic Life*, p. 150.

at L'Abri, the image of Fran as a "missionary to intellectuals" was born.

Fran was something of a reluctant celebrity. He was by nature an introvert, even though he loved spending time with people and talking to them about Jesus. The lifestyle of L'Abri, with its lack of privacy and personal space, was difficult for him in many ways. He didn't seek out the limelight; just as he had resisted those early tape recordings, he continued to be cautious about each new step that would lead to more publicity.

By popular request, in 1965 Fran began to make more trips back to the United States, to give lectures and lead discussions. Initially, American evangelicals were quite taken aback by the unusual sight of this little man with his long hair and goatee beard, wearing the "funny" Swiss clothes he had adopted of knickerbockers, long socks and hiking boots. They were even more surprised when he began to speak to them about modern art, films and popular music, which many Christians had been brought up to avoid. Fran's method of reaching out to unbelievers involved understanding their worldview, and for him that meant engaging with popular culture rather than pretending it didn't exist. The 1960s was a decade of rapid change and breaking with "tradition", a time when young people were questioning everything. It was a decade of protests; protests over America's involvement in the Vietnam War, protests over civil rights, protests over freedom of speech. Francis Schaeffer's approach was exactly what the evangelical world needed. He taught Christians how to connect with people and show that the Bible's message was as true and relevant then as ever. Fran's ideas met with an enthusiastic response, and he was asked to develop a series of lectures he gave at Wheaton College into a book that could be published. Again, he resisted initially but began to see that it would further the cause of the gospel. Thus his first book, "The God Who is There" was written, and published in 1968 along with his second, "Escape from Reason." They would be the first of more than twenty books and booklets published over Fran's lifetime.

"We had been willing to remain in a chalet on a mountainside and pray for the ones of the Lord's choice to come to us there," Edith later wrote. "The time came when we realized we must open ourselves also to being willing to go wherever the Lord wanted to take us to the people He might want us to speak to."[2] The new direction their ministry was taking was costly for her too, as it often meant leaving her family behind to travel alongside Fran, or else extended times apart. There was a real spiritual struggle taking place within her during the early 1960s, as the demands on Fran were just beginning to increase. "I had begun to look away from 'willingness for anything' to a desire for 'something for myself', and this filled far too much of my thoughts and prayer times,"[3] she admitted.

---

2. *The Tapestry*, p. 519.

3. Ibid, p. 519.

One evening, Edith was with Fran in Zurich, at the apartment of a Christian air hostess who had invited him along to speak to some of her non-Christian friends. Edith sat in the corner sipping tea and admiring the "arty" decor of the room as it filled up with pilots and airline staff, doctors, lawyers and businessmen. From her quiet corner, Edith watched their faces as they asked Fran their questions about the Christian faith. As Fran spoke to them, she saw how their expressions slowly changed from scorn and scepticism to curiosity, surprise and real interest. And as she saw this, she began to pray, silently. "Oh Lord, please forgive me if I have been a piece of dirt in the water-pipe. Forgive me if I have hindered the work of your Spirit in any way. If you want Fran to do a much wider work, if you want what happened here in this room tonight to happen on a much larger scale, if you have people in other parts of the world who should hear what Fran has said tonight ... then I am willing for whatever it takes on my part. Forgive me for my selfish prayers for a different life. I promise I'll go on, as you give me strength, to do whatever my part requires."[4]

Edith's "part", as ever, would be no small one.

"In many ways, she was the secret of L'Abri."[5]

"As many people were brought to the Lord through Mrs. Schaeffer's cinnamon buns as through Dr. Schaeffer's sermons!"[6]

---

4. Ibid, p. 520.

5. Os Guiness, quoted in Duriez, *Francis Schaeffer*, p.71.

6. Mary Pride, *The Way Home* (Home Life Books, 1985), p. 202.

These were the kind of things people close to the Schaeffers would observe about Edith. It was only through her considerable homemaking skills, such as her organization, cooking and hospitality, that an endeavour such as L'Abri was even possible. Yet her role was certainly not confined to the kitchen. God had blessed Edith with unusual energy and stamina, and after busy days of taking care of the family and guests, she would often work long into the night, typing letters, and later the manuscripts of her own books. Many admired her for her energy, although sometimes those around her felt as though they were struggling to keep up. It could be said that the intense, unpredictable lifestyle of L'Abri suited her personality better than it did Fran's, for Edith thrived on busyness.

Since childhood, Edith had also been learning from her parents and other missionaries how to talk to people about God. She was well read and, more importantly, had a deep personal relationship with the Lord. There were many times when people came to her to talk through their problems and questions, both at L'Abri and elsewhere. However, she soon had to make sure that she wasn't "indispensable" to the running of L'Abri. Fran and Edith had never forgotten his exhaustion after that first three month trip around Europe so many years before, and as much as possible Edith tried to travel alongside him when he later went on long speaking tours to America, the U.K. and other places, so that she could support him and take care of his needs. Then it was her responsibility to make sure that the L'Abri workers were able to keep things going in their absence.

As Fran's fame grew, Edith also had many opportunities to speak publicly and to write. Many people were fascinated by the Schaeffers' experiences, and in 1969 Edith's first book "L'Abri" was published, telling the gripping story of how God had brought them to Switzerland and of all that happened there in that little mountain village of Huémoz. Lots of women naturally came to see Edith as a role model and eagerly read her later books on family and homemaking, but she would also go on to write about issues such as the place of Jews within the Christian church, and the endurance of suffering. Fran supported her fully and would always say that their books should be taken together as a body of work.

On a personal level, Fran also depended on Edith completely. That was why he found traveling without her so hard and needed her at his side. The book of Genesis describes Eve, Adam's wife, as being a "helper suitable for him". Edith was Fran's helper in every way. She supported him both practically and emotionally. Her strength and her unwavering belief in him made it possible for Fran to keep going in the work God had given him to do.

Never Retired

Francis Schaeffer's books were selling in their millions, and had been translated into twenty-five languages. He was constantly in demand to give lectures and lead discussions, in cities and at universities all over the world. In the meantime, the L'Abri work continued to thrive. One day, his son Franky, now grown up, came to his father with a new suggestion.

"Dad," he said, earnestly. "You're saying something different, something that people want to hear. I've been wondering if you would consider doing a film? That way you could reach an even wider audience."

Fran took time to think and pray over this idea carefully. He instinctively felt reluctant, but he was pleased to see Franky's enthusiasm. His son had long had an interest in film-making, and Fran wanted to encourage him. In all honesty, he often felt guilty about Franky and the lack of time he had spent with his son over the last few years, with the endless writing and speaking tours. Franky had been so tiny when the L'Abri work began, and it hadn't always been easy for him. Working together on a project could be good for their relationship. Besides, his son was right – it might be a way to reach even more people with the gospel. Fran himself had long been aware of the power of film to communicate ideas.

Over the next few years, Fran and his son would work together on two separate film series', entitled "How Should We Then Live?" and "Whatever Happened To The Human Race?" The second particularly addressed the issues of abortion and euthanasia, emphasizing the value of human life. This came after the decision of the U.S. Supreme Court in 1973 to allow every woman the right to an abortion in the first three months of pregnancy. For Fran to tackle such a controversial political issue was quite a new step for him. It represented his growing desire to help people come to know Jesus not only as their Savior but also as their Lord – Lord over every aspect of life. The focus of some of his later work moved towards social and political issues, because he wanted Christians to see that faith was connected to the whole of life. He encouraged Christians to be more proactive in their defence of biblical values, and this had a massive impact on the American evangelical world during the 1970s and 80s.

Fran and Edith, by now in their early sixties, found the months of filming gruelling even by their standards. Scenes were shot in a variety of different locations, involving a lot of traveling, long hours and broken nights. As the filming of the second series went on,

Edith grew more and more concerned about Fran's tiredness and weight loss. Was it simply the result of their punishing schedule – or was there something else going on? Back in Switzerland, the family noticed that Fran's coat no longer fitted him, and when he weighed himself Fran found that he had lost twenty-five pounds.

As soon as they were able, Fran and Edith flew to the Mayo Clinic in Rochester, Minnesota. Fran was admitted to the clinic for tests while Edith spent an anxious night alone at a nearby hotel. As she lay awake, tossing and turning in the unfamiliar bed, Edith turned to the Savior who had been her constant refuge through so many ups and downs. While she prayed for God to make Fran well, she still remembered to look for His blessings, the signs of His loving care even in the midst of this trial.

"Oh Lord," she prayed, "I know that it is right to give thanks in all things. Thank you so much for that comfortable room Fran has in the clinic. Thank you for the blue and white curtains and the painting on the wall … and most of all for the phone beside his bed that has allowed us to talk and pray together even tonight. Thank you … "

The test results showed that it was cancer. Fran telephoned each of his children in turn to break the news. His treatment began immediately, and he and Edith had to move temporarily into a small apartment near the clinic. However, if anyone had expected that this might mark the beginning of Dr. Schaeffer's retirement, they were much mistaken! When Fran arrived at the Mayo clinic, he was surprised by how many of the doctors knew of his work and had even read his books. Later he described to a friend how opportunities had arisen even in those most unlikely circumstances.

"It was rather humorous really. The doctors would always say, 'Now you're here to get well and not to work', which was inevitably followed by a 'but' something. This time it was, 'but will you show two episodes of "How Should We Then Live?" every Sunday night and then lead a discussion, with mics on the floor?' I didn't know if I could do it, because I was right in the middle of the most strenuous part of chemotherapy. But we prayed about it, and I decided to. They thought there might be two or three hundred people turn up. That first night there were 1,500."[1]

Before long, the decision was made to open a L'Abri center right there in Rochester, so that Fran and Edith would be able to continue their ministry as much as possible. Yet they still regarded Swiss L'Abri as their home, and always would. After several months of treatment, Fran's cancer went into a short remission, but a few months later he was embarking on another course of chemotherapy. This time he was able to have drug treatment, which enabled him to travel, both home to Huémoz but also elsewhere as he continued

---

1. Duriez, *Francis Schaeffer*, p. 197.

to speak publicly, often leading seminars which followed showings of episodes from the films. He was determined to finish the book he was working on, "The Church at the End of the Twentieth Century." He also spent many hours revising several of his other books, ready for the publication of his five volume "Complete Works", which was completed in 1982, four years into his cancer battle.

In the early spring of 1984, increasingly weak and frail, Fran embarked on what would be his final speaking tour. He visited thirteen cities. At times he had to be carried on a stretcher to the location of the talk, but he would not stop: he felt he still had so much to say, and to do.

"I'm late, I'm late, I'm going to miss the plane. Where are my notes?"

There was panic in Fran's voice as he tried to lift himself from the bed, hands scrabbling around on the white sheets.

"Dad."

Susan clasped his trembling hands in her own, marvelling at the fragility of them. Those hands that had been so big, so strong; workman's hands.

"Dad, you are not going to speak," she said, quietly. Their eyes met.

"But I have to do it ... " The words trailed away.

"No, Dad." Susan's voice was gentle, but firm. "You're going to rest now. Your work is over."

His big, brown, sad eyes focused on her own, and understood. The work – or rather his part in it – was done.

Francis Schaeffer died on the May 15th, 1984. Edith wrote movingly about that day:

It was at 4:00 am precisely that a soft last breath was taken ... and he was absent. That absence was so sharp and precise! Absent. Now I only observed the absence. As for his presence with the Lord ... I had to turn to my BIBLE to know that. I only know that a person is present with the Lord because the Bible tells us so. I did not have a mystical experience. I want to tell you here and now that the inerrant Bible became more important to me than ever before. I want to tell you very seriously and solemnly ... the Bible is more precious than ever to me. My husband fought for truth and fought for the truth of the inspiration of the Bible – the inerrancy of the Bible – all the days that I knew him ... through my 52 years of knowing him. But – never have I been more impressed with the wonder of having a trustworthy message from God, an unshakable word from God – than right then![2]

Edith took immeasurable comfort from knowing that her beloved husband was now with Jesus. He was safe forever with the Lord he had loved and followed, wholeheartedly, since the age of seventeen. In her grief

---

2. Edith Schaeffer, Dear Family: *The L'Abri Family Letters*, (Harper & Row, 1989), p. 388.

she stood firmly upon the sure foundation of the truths of the Bible, the truths she and Fran had spent their lives defending.

More than eight hundred people poured into the auditorium of the John Marshall High School in Rochester to attend Fran's funeral. On an enormous screen, they watched the fifth episode of "Whatever Happened to the Human Race?", seeing and hearing Dr. Schaeffer himself doing what he loved best, speaking about the meaning and power of Christ and His resurrection. Mourners shed tears as they were reminded of God's wonderful promise in the book of Revelation, that one day there would be no more tears. They listened to the very words Debby had read aloud to the family on the day he died: "He will wipe every tear from their eyes. There will be no more death or mourning or crying or pain, for the old order of things has passed away" (Revelation 21:4 NIV).

As Edith herself recognized, it was "far better" for Fran. The sorrow was for those left behind.

* * *

Fiona Macaulay admired the long bob her grandmother had just had cut. It was a big change for her after a lifetime of wearing her hair long, tied up in a bun. Even now, her "Nony" looked stylish and youthful, full of her usual energy and zest for life.

"Somehow you never seem 'old', like other people do, Nony!" Fiona laughed, as they strolled beside the tranquil waters of the lake at Montreux, a spot Fran and

Edith had loved to visit together. It was 1991, and the whole family had gathered together for a big reunion. It still felt strange without Fran, and they were all very aware of his absence. Even his coat still hung beside the door of Edith's house.

Now, the "old" lady smiled at her granddaughter's words.

"On my thirteenth birthday, I remember waking up and realizing I felt no different to when I was twelve!" she replied, with a twinkle in her eye. "That's just the way it has always been. I still want to live life to the full."

And she did. Although she grieved for the loss of her husband, Edith knew that God had left her behind for a reason; that He is the one who "numbers our days". As long as she was able, she continued to serve God with all the gifts he had given her; through hospitality, through talking to people, through writing. In her widowhood, God also opened up new ways for Edith to serve him.

After Fran's death, a friend of L'Abri gave Edith some money to buy a used Steinway grand piano in his memory, knowing how much the Schaeffers both loved art and music of all kinds. During the process of finding one to buy, Edith became very interested in Steinway and travelled to New York City to research and write a book called "Forever Music." This led her into a particular ministry to musicians and artists, whom she would invite to her home in Rochester and to L'Abri to share their gifts with others. She also wrote other books, including one on prayer. A lifetime of seeing God answer prayers – not always with the expected, or even the desired answer, but in His Sovereign wisdom – had given her a lot of experience to share with others.

To celebrate her eightieth birthday, Edith travelled back to her birthplace of Wenzhou, China, accompanied by her daughter-in-law Genie, Franky's wife. It was a trip she had longed to make for many years, for China had always been close to her heart. Indeed, the memories of her early childhood there were so fresh that in her old age she wrote a children's book about them, entitled: "Mei Fuh: Memories of China". Remarkably, despite the impact of the communist regime upon the country, Edith found the mission compound virtually unchanged, and she was able to walk around the buildings and the dusty courtyard she remembered so well.

In the last ten years of her life, Edith sold the house in Rochester and moved permanently back to Switzerland. Here her daughter Debby and her husband Udo oversaw her care as her eyesight deteriorated and she began to suffer some memory loss. She lived next door to them in a chalet that was aptly named "Mon Abri"; "my shelter". Despite the memory loss, Edith could always recite hymns and passages of Scripture. She was surrounded by the artwork of her son Franky. She loved to watch the BBC and to be read aloud to from the favorite books of her childhood like "Anne of Green Gables." And when she could no longer remember all the names of her grandchildren, and great-grandchildren, she would ask her carers to read out all their names so that she could pray for each one.

Edith Schaeffer was unwavering in her faith to the very end. She went to be with her risen Lord on Easter weekend, March 30th, 2013, aged ninety-eight years old.

Postscript

Following Francis Schaeffer's death, President Ronald Reagan wrote these words in a letter to the family: "He will long be remembered as one of the great Christian thinkers of our century." The well-known evangelist Billy Graham described him as "truly one of the great evangelical statesmen of our generation." Edith Schaeffer was included in Helen Kooiman Hosier's "100 Christian Women who Changed the Twentieth Century."

Yet personal fame was not what Fran and Edith Schaeffer set out to achieve, and no doubt they will be best remembered by the many individuals who came to faith through their witness. Those who were blessed by their time, their hospitality, their wisdom, and their love for people. Those who came to know Christ because of their generous and sacrificial giving of themselves, following the example of the Savior who lay down His life for sinners.

Those of us who did not meet the Schaeffers can still be inspired by their example and their teaching, thanks to their many books. If you would like to read more about them, Edith Schaeffer's "L'Abri" would be a good place to start.

The ministry of "L'Abri" continues today, in the original location in Huémoz, Switzerland, as well as in several other branches throughout Europe, America and Asia. These are primarily residential study centers, open to anyone, which seek to maintain the informal, family atmosphere that was so important to the "L'Abri" of the Schaeffers. They continue to be founded upon the objective truths of Christianity as clearly laid down in the Bible.

Recommended Reading

About the Schaeffers

L'Abri by Edith Schaeffer (Crossway Books, revised edition 1992; first published 1969)

Francis Schaeffer: An Authentic Life by Colin Duriez (Crossway, 2008)

About the Christian Faith

A Sneaking Suspicion by John Dickson (Matthias Media, first published 1992)

The Case for Christ for Kids by Lee Strobel (Zonderkidz, 2010)

The Case for Christ, Student Edition by Lee Strobel (Zondervan, 2014)

The Bible is God's Word: The Evidence by Catherine Mackenzie (CF4Kids, Revised edition 2015)

Thinking Further Topics

Chapter One: A Meeting of Minds

What was it that attracted Francis and Edith to one another? Think about the idea of romantic relationships many people have. Do you think Christians should approach romantic relationships differently; if so, how?

Chapter Two: Fran

Trace the way that God worked in Fran's life to bring him to the point of accepting Jesus. What was it about the Bible that rang true for Fran? Think about your own experience of reading the Bible. Have you found the answers to your questions? Fran didn't have anyone to help him understand the Bible at that time, but most of us do. If you aren't sure whether the Bible has the answers to your questions, why not talk to a Christian you know. You could also get hold of one of the titles on our "Recommended Reading" list at the back of this book.

Chapter Three: Changing Course

Fran's parents didn't understand his new faith and didn't want him to pursue a career in Christian ministry. How did he respond to their opposition?

Do you think he did the right thing? Think about your own relationship with your parents. How can you honor them even when you disagree on things?

Chapter Four: Edith

How did Edith's faith in Jesus grow and develop through her childhood? Think back through your own life. Can you see how God used certain people or experiences to draw you to Himself? Give thanks for those things. Remembering what God has done for us is a vital part of our Christian lives and will help us to keep going when we're finding it hard.

Chapter Five: Learning and Longing

How did Fran earn the respect of his neighbors at college? How did he use the opportunities he had to share the gospel? Think about where God has put you and how you could reach out to those who don't know Jesus. How is Fran's example an encouragement? Pray that God would give you opportunities to speak about Him.

Chapter Six: Together or Apart?

What do you think troubled Fran about his relationship with Edith? How did they make sure they honored God in their relationship? Think about your own life and the things that are most important you to you – maybe a friend, a relationship, or a hobby. Is there anything in your life that is more important to you than God? Pray that God will help you enjoy his good gifts while loving the Giver most of all.

Chapter Seven: For Better and For Worse

What were some of the difficulties Fran and Edith experienced in their early married life? What were some of the blessings? Why is it important to remember that Christians are forgiven sinners or "works in progress"? Think about how that might improve our relationships with other Christians, whether friends, family members or others in our churches.

Chapter Eight: Ministry in America

How do you think Fran felt when his father became a Christian? How does this encourage us to keep praying for others?

Think about how Edith deals with uncertainty at the end of the chapter. Are there any areas of your life right now where you feel the need of God's guidance? How could you follow her example?

Chapter Nine: To St Louis and Beyond

How was the summer of Fran's trip to Europe a testing time, both for him and for the family at home? Fran suffered a breakdown when he returned home. What do you think he might have learned from this experience, about himself and about God? It might help to look at 2 Corinthians 11: 27-30 and 12:9-10.

Chapter Ten: A Nomadic Life

What made the decision to leave America particularly hard for the Schaeffers? What challenges did they face during their early months in Europe, and how did they make the best of them?

Think about the challenges or difficulties you are facing at the moment. Ask God for his help to trust Him in them.

Chapter Eleven: Move to the Mountains

What opportunities did Fran and Edith have to share the gospel in Champéry?

Notice how often the Schaeffers invited people into their home and showed them hospitality. How do you think that made their witness to Christ more effective?

Chapter Twelve: Fair Skies and Dark Clouds

This chapter describes some of the trials and discouragements the Schaeffer family faced. How should we react when we face such trials? What promises in the Bible could we hold on to? (If you're not sure, start with Romans 8: 28-39!)

Chapter Thirteen: Living by Faith

How do the Schaeffers experience answered prayer in this chapter? How might this encourage you to persevere with prayer?

Fran went through a period of questioning his faith during his time at Chalet Bijou. What can we learn from how he dealt with his doubts? How did he emerge from it better equipped to help others?

Chapter Fourteen: L'Abri

Look at the four main principles about how L'Abri would be run. Why do you think Fran and Edith chose to do things this way?

What do you find particularly exciting or encouraging about Jane's story?

Chapter Fifteen: The Work Grows

Fran and Edith wanted the work at L'Abri to proceed according to God's plan, not their own. How do we see that happening in this chapter? Does this mean Christians shouldn't make plans? (It might help to read James 4: 13-15).

Pray for the unfolding of God's plan in your own life.

Chapter Sixteen: Into the Limelight

Why do you think Fran was a "reluctant celebrity"? What do you think some of the challenges of fame might be, for a Christian?

Think about Edith's contribution to the Schaeffer's ministry. How did she use the gifts God had given her? She and Fran were very different people. How do you think God used their differences to make them a good team?

It is easy to feel intimidated by the example of other Christians who seem to be far more gifted or hard-working than we are! Sometimes people felt intimidated by Edith, particularly because of her unusual energy. However, in her books Edith often reminded her readers that she and Fran were far from perfect. God has deliberately made us all different, with different strengths and weaknesses.

Read 1 Corinthians 12: 12-27. How does the picture of the church as a body help us to understand why God made us all different? Think and pray about your own strengths and weaknesses. Thank God for the gifts he has given you, and pray for opportunities to use them to serve Him.

Chapter Seventeen: Never Retired

How did Fran and Edith continue to honor God as they faced illness, old age and ultimately death?

Now that you have finished the book, think about what stands out to you most about the lives of Francis and Edith Schaeffer. How might their example spur you on in your Christian life? Think about what you have learned about God through their story. Remember, their God is our God too! He is the God of the Bible, whom we can know personally today.

Francis and Edith Schaeffer Timeline

1912	Francis Schaeffer born in Germantown, Philadelphia.
1914	Edith Seville born in Wenzhou, China.
1919	The Seville family return to the U.S.A.
1930	Francis Schaeffer ("Fran") converted to Christ at an evangelistic tent meeting.
1931	Fran goes to Hampden-Sydney college as a ministerial student.
1932	Fran and Edith meet and begin a relationship.
1935	Fran and Edith get married; Fran begins seminary.
1937	Their first child, Priscilla, is born.
1938	Fran becomes a pastor in Grove City, Pennsylvania.
1939-45	World War II.
1947	Fran makes a tour of post-war Europe.
1948	The Schaeffer family relocate to Europe under the Independent Board of Presbyterian Foreign Missions.
1949	The family move to Champéry, Switzerland.
1955	The family move to Chalet les Mélèzes, Huémoz and begin "L'Abri".
1955-75	The Vietnam War.
1958	Fran and Edith make their first trip to England.

1959   *Time* magazine publish an article about L'Abri.

1963   Assassination of President John F. Kennedy.

1964-65   Free Speech Movement: student protests at the University of California, Berkeley.

1965   Francis Schaeffer begins to make regular trips back to the U.S. to speak and lecture publicly.

1968   Publication of *The God Who Is There* and *Escape from Reason*.

1969   Publication of Edith's first book, *L'Abri*.

1973   U.S. Supreme Court decision to legalise abortion.

1976-77   *How Should We Then Live?* book and accompanying film series is released.

1978   Francis Schaeffer diagnosed with a type of cancer called lymphoma.

1979   *Whatever Happened to the Human Race?* book and film released.

1984   Death of Francis Schaeffer, aged seventy-two.

1986-00   Edith Schaeffer writes a further ten books. She continues to host people in her home and speak about the Lord Jesus, both privately and publicly.

1994   Edith celebrates her eightieth birthday with a five month trip to China, to visit her birthplace.

2013   Death of Edith Schaeffer, aged ninety-eight.

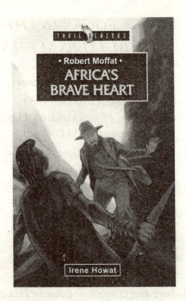

Robert Moffat: Africa's Brave Heart
by Irene Howat

Robert Moffat could think on his feet, and use his hands. He was strong, practical and just the sort of guy you needed to back you up when you were in difficulty. Not only that, he had courage — loads of it, and a longing to bring the good news of Jesus Christ to the people of Africa.

As Robert faced the dangers of drought, wild animals and even the daggers and spears of the people he had come to help, he used his unique collection of gifts and attributes to spread the gospel.

Africa's brave heart blazed a trail into the unknown, starting a work in that continent that continues today.

ISBN: 978-1-84550-715-2

OTHER BOOKS IN THE
TRAIL BLAZERS SERIES

Augustine, The Truth Seeker
ISBN 978-1-78191-296-6
John Calvin, After Darkness Light
ISBN 978-1-78191-550-9
Fanny Crosby, The Blind Girl's Song
ISBN 978-1-78191-163-1
John Knox, The Sharpened Sword
ISBN 978-1-78191-057-3
Eric Liddell, Finish the Race
ISBN 978-1-84550-590-5
Martin Luther, Reformation Fire
ISBN 978-1-78191-521-9
Robert Moffat, Africa's Brave Heart
ISBN 978-1-84550-715-2
D.L. Moody, One Devoted Man
ISBN 978-1-78191-676-6
Mary of Orange, At the Mercy of Kings
ISBN 978-1-84550-818-0
Patrick of Ireland: The Boy who Forgave
ISBN: 978-1-78191-677-3
John Stott, The Humble Leader
ISBN 978-1-84550-787-9
Ulrich Zwingli, Shepherd Warrior
ISBN 978-1-78191-803-6

**For a full list of Trail Blazers, please see our
website: www.christianfocus.com
All Trail Blazers are available as e-books**